Buckle Down!®

on
Mathematics

Level 3

This book belongs to: _____

*Helping the schoolhouse meet the
standards of the statehouse*™

Buckle Down
PUBLISHING COMPANY

ISBN 0-7836-2563-4

Catalog #BD US3M 1   2 3 4 5 6 7 8 9 10

President and Publisher: Douglas J. Paul, Ph.D.; Editorial Director: John Hansen; Senior Editor: Doria Knebel; Project Editor: Michael J. Morony; Editors: Todd Hamer, Paul Meyers; Production Editor: Michael Hankes; Production Director: Jennifer Booth; Production Supervisor: Ginny York; Art Director: Chris Wolf; Graphic Designer: Carla Peterson.

Cover image: © Corbis

TABLE OF CONTENTS

INTRODUCTION

How much math do you know? You probably know a lot—even if it doesn't always seem that way. You have been using math for years. And every year, you add more to what you already know.

Learning to solve math problems is a lot like learning to play a new video game. You need to know what steps to take to stay in the game and come up with the right answers. Math can be a lot of fun if you know what you are doing. How do you get better at math? You practice. And the more you practice, the better you will get.

How This Book Can Help

Buckle Down on Mathematics, Level 3, will give you lots of practice to help you do your best at math. Each lesson teaches important math skills. There are also some tips to help you become a better math problem-solver.

Test-Taking Tips

Here are a few tips that will help you on test day.

TIP 1: Take it easy.

Because you've practiced the problems in *Buckle Down*, you will be ready to do your best on almost any math test. You can do it!

TIP 2: Have what you need.

For most math tests, you will need a few sharp pencils, an eraser, and a calculator. Your teacher will tell you if you need anything else.

TIP 3: Read the harder questions more than once.

Every question is different. Some are short, some are long. Some are easy, some are hard. If you need to, read the harder ones more than once. This will help you make a plan.

TIP 4: Learn to "plug in" answers to multiple-choice questions.

When do you "plug in"? You should "plug in" whenever your answer is different from all of the answer choices or you can't come up with an answer. Plug each answer choice into the problem and find the one that makes sense. (You can also think of this as "working backwards.")

TIP 5: Answer every question.

Do your best to answer every question. If you don't have the answer, it's OK to guess. You might get it right!

TIP 6: Use all the test time.

Work on the test until you are told to stop. If you finish early, double-check your answers.

Number Sense, Numeration, and Numerical Operations

Numbers are used for just about everything. You use numbers when you put candles on a birthday cake, keep score on a video game, or make a pitcher of juice. You use huge numbers to say how far it is to the planet Pluto or how hot the sun is. You use tiny numbers to tell how long an ant is or how much a butterfly weighs.

In this unit, you will do all kinds of things with all kinds of numbers—from big numbers like 9,999 to small numbers like $\frac{1}{9}$. You will read, write, compare, add, subtract, multiply, and divide numbers. You will work with numbers written as fractions, mixed numbers, and decimals. Along the way, you will learn about number properties and how to solve story problems.

In This Unit

Whole Numbers

Fractions and Mixed Numbers

Computation and Number Properties

Problem Solving

Lesson 1

Whole Numbers

Numbers are used to describe "how many" of something there is. Some of the numbers (0, 1, 2, 3, and so on) are known as **whole numbers**. There are different ways to show whole numbers. You can use digits, words, or drawings.

Digits

The digits 0, 1, 2, 3, 4, 5, 6, 7, 8, and 9 are used to write whole numbers.

The number 1,324 has four digits (1, 3, 2, and 4).

When you use digits to write numbers, you can write the numbers in **standard** or **expanded** form.

> **Standard form:** 1,324

> **Expanded form:** 1,000 + 300 + 20 + 4

Words

Write down a number as you would say it out loud.

1,324 can be written in words as "one thousand, three hundred twenty-four."

Drawings

1,324 can be shown in a drawing like this.

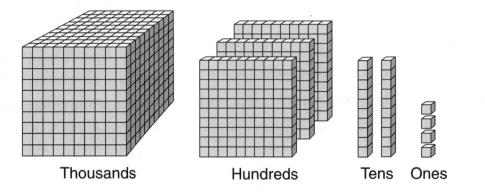

Thousands   Hundreds   Tens   Ones

PRACTICE

Directions: Use the drawing to answer Numbers 1 through 3.

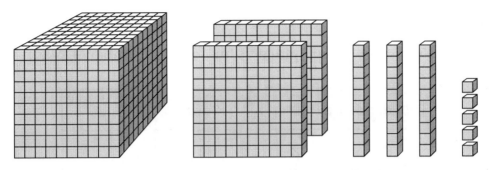

1. Write the number in **standard form**. _____

2. Write the number in **expanded form**. _____

3. Write the number in **words**.

_____

4. Write your own four-digit number. _____ , _____ _____ _____

Write your number in **expanded form**.

_____

Write your number in **words**.

_____

5. How is seven hundred eighty-four written in standard form?

   A.   7.804

   B.   78.4

   C.   784

   D. 7,840

6. How is 5,607 written in words?

   A. fifty-six seven

   B. fifty-six hundred seven

   C. five hundred sixty-seven

   D. five thousand, six hundred seven

Place Value

Place value helps you understand the value of each digit in a number.

EXAMPLE

The table shows each place value for the number 9,241.

Thousands	Hundreds	Tens	Ones
9	2	4	1

9,000   +   200   +   40   +   1

PRACTICE

1. Write this number in the following table: 3,000 + 400 + 50 + 5.

Thousands	Hundreds	Tens	Ones

2. Write a number with a 6 in the thousands place, a 2 in the hundreds place, a 7 in the tens place, and a 3 in the ones place.

Thousands	Hundreds	Tens	Ones

3. Write three different numbers in this place-value table.

Thousands	Hundreds	Tens	Ones

Now write the numbers from the table in expanded form.

_____

_____

_____

Directions: Use the table to answer Numbers 4 and 5.

Thousands	Hundreds	Tens	Ones
7	5	2	8

4. What is the value of the 7?

   A.   7
   B.   70
   C.   700
   D. 7,000

5. What is the value of the 2?

   A.   2
   B.   20
   C.   200
   D. 2,000

Even and Odd Numbers

To find even or odd numbers, look at the **last** digit of the number.

EXAMPLES

Even numbers end in 0, 2, 4, 6, or 8.   **634**

The last digit of 634 is 4. The number 634 is even.

Odd numbers end in 1, 3, 5, 7, or 9.   **781**

The last digit of 781 is 1. The number 781 is odd.

PRACTICE

Directions: Write the letter **E** if the number is even or **O** if the number is odd in Numbers 1 and 2.

1. 70 _____   972 _____   7 _____

2. 135 _____   1,357 _____   2,948 _____

3. Write your own even number. Use 4 digits.

_____ ,   _____   _____   _____

4. Write your own odd number. Use 4 digits.

_____ ,   _____   _____   _____

5. Which of the following is an odd number?

   A. 1,416
   B. 4,871
   C. 5,342
   D. 8,294

6. Which of the following is an even number?

   A. 29,151
   B. 33,333
   C. 62,199
   D. 76,714

Comparing and Ordering Numbers

When you compare numbers, you use words like these:

smaller than	the smallest
less than	the least
fewer than	the fewest
greater than	the greatest
larger than	the largest
more than	the most
equal to	the same

You can also use **symbols** to compare numbers.

$>$	means **is greater than**
$<$	means **is less than**
$=$	means **is equal to**

Think of the symbols $>$ and $<$ as the open mouth of a hungry fish. The fish will **always** swim to the bigger number and eat it.

EXAMPLE

Compare 10 and 15.

10 is less than 15.

$10 < 15$

15 is greater than 10.

$15 > 10$

Another way to compare numbers is to write them in a place-value table.

EXAMPLE

Which number is greater, 8,235 or 8,214?

Step 1: **Write the numbers in a place-value table.**

Thousands	Hundreds	Tens	Ones
8	2	3	5
8	2	1	4

Step 2: **Start from the left column and compare the digits until they are different.**

Are the numbers in the thousands and hundreds column the same or different?

They are the same, so look at the numbers in the tens column.

Which number has more tens?

3 tens > 1 ten

Step 3: **Order the numbers.** Write the correct symbols.

8,235 > 8,214   or   8,214 < 8,235

PRACTICE

Directions: Use this list to answer Numbers 1 through 4.

TICKETS SOLD

Lauren	57
Alfie	123
Gerard	29
Forrest	146

1. Write the numbers from the list in the place-value table.

Tickets Sold

Hundreds	Tens	Ones

2. Who sold the most tickets?

   _____

3. Use the symbol > or < to compare the numbers.

   57 _____ 29

   57 _____ 123

   146 _____ 123

4. Which list shows the numbers in order from **greatest** to **least**?

   A. 57, 123, 29, 146

   B. 123, 57, 146, 29

   C. 29, 57, 123, 146

   D. 146, 123, 57, 29

TEST YOUR SKILLS

1. Ms. Connor is ordering from a tile company. She needs 275 tiles. How do you write this number in words?

   A. twenty-five hundred seventy-five thousand
   B. twenty-five hundred seventy-five
   C. two thousand, seventy-five
   D. two hundred seventy-five

2. How is nine hundred forty-five written in standard form?

   A.   905
   B.   945
   C.   954
   D. 9,045

3. What is the standard form for 1,000 + 400 + 30 + 2?

   A.   132
   B.   1,432
   C.   14,032
   D. 1,000,400,302

4. Which number has an 8 in the tens place?

   A. 8,134
   B.   844
   C.   687
   D.   308

5. One day, Miss West counted six hundred two birds flying south. How do you write that number in standard form?

   A. 602
   B. 206
   C. 62
   D. 26

6. What number is missing in this expanded form of 396?

   396 = ? + 90 + 6

   A.   3
   B.   30
   C.   300
   D. 3,000

7. Which list of numbers is ordered from **least** to **greatest**?

   A. 798, 897, 890
   B. 119, 124, 221
   C. 853, 358, 530
   D. 331, 449, 448

8. Which of the following shows an odd number of objects?

A.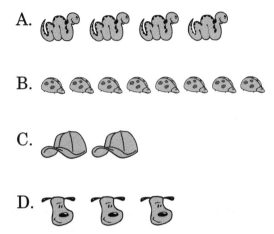

B.

C.

D.

9. This drawing shows the number of tires made at a factory in one hour.

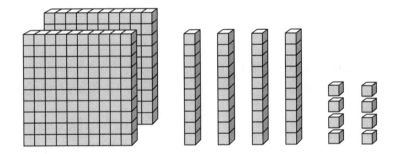

How many tires are made at the factory in one hour?

A. 248
B. 484
C. 524
D. 842

10. Mary Sue has 139 books on her bookshelf. Ricky has 147. Who has **more** books than Mary Sue but **fewer** books than Ricky?

A. Kelvin − 130 books
B. Susie − 148 books
C. Liz − 142 books
D. Eric − 139 books

11. Compare the numbers.

    86 _____ 92

    A. <
    B. >
    C. =
    D. ÷

12. Which of the following is an even number?

    A. 261
    B. 513
    C. 749
    D. 836

13. What is the value of the 5 in the following number?

    2,586

    A. 5,000
    B.   500
    C.   50
    D.   5

14. What is the expanded form of 6,079?

    A. 6,000 + 700 + 90
    B. 6,000 + 700 + 9
    C. 6,000 + 70 + 9
    D. 6,000 + 7 + 9

15. What is the largest whole number you can make using the digits 5, 2, 8, and 3? Use each digit exactly once.

    A. 5,283
    B. 8,523
    C. 5,832
    D. 8,532

16. Which number is the greatest, 832, 467, 903, or 752?

    A. 832
    B. 467
    C. 903
    D. 752

17. How is 3,257 written in words?

    A. three thousand, two hundred fifty-seven
    B. three hundred twenty-five seven
    C. three thousand, two hundred seventy-five
    D. three and two hundred fifty-seven

18. Which number has a 4 in the ones place?

    A. 7,492
    B. 9,274
    C. 4,927
    D. 2,749

 **Lesson 2**

Fractions and Mixed Numbers

Fractions and mixed numbers are numbers that are not whole.

Fractions

A **fraction** names a part of a whole or a part of a set.

EXAMPLES

This window is divided into 4 equal parts. $\frac{1}{4}$ of the window is broken. $\frac{3}{4}$ is not broken. In words, $\frac{1}{4}$ is read "one-fourth"; $\frac{3}{4}$ is read "three-fourths."

Each sock is 1 part of a pair. The fraction $\frac{1}{2}$ names 1 part of the set of 2. In words, $\frac{1}{2}$ is read "one-half."

The **numerator** tells how many **parts** of the whole or set **you have**.

The **denominator** tells how many **parts** the whole or set **is divided into**.

$$\textbf{numerator} \rightarrow \frac{1}{7} \leftarrow \textbf{denominator}$$

numerator → $\frac{1}{7}$

denominator → 7

➡ **TIP:** The **D**enominator is **D**ownstairs.

PRACTICE

Directions: Use the following pictures to answer Numbers 1 through 4.

1. How many sharks are shaded? _____

2. How many sharks are shown in all? _____

3. Write the fraction that shows the number of shaded sharks. _____

4. What is the word name for the fraction that shows the number of sharks that are **not** shaded?

    A. three
    B. four
    C. thirty-four
    D. three-fourths

5. What is the fraction that names the shaded parts of the circle?

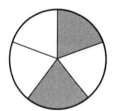

    A. $\frac{2}{5}$

    B. $\frac{3}{5}$

    C. $\frac{2}{3}$

    D. $\frac{5}{2}$

6. Count the number of points on this star. Then, draw dots on the end of 3 of its points.

   Now write the fraction that tells how many points of the star have dots on their ends.

   _____

7. What fraction names 2 parts of this set of 3? _____

8. Color some of the squares in the following rectangle. Then write the fraction that names the colored squares.

   _____

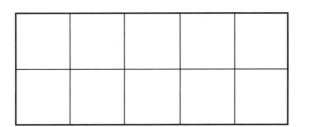

Equivalent Forms of Fractions

Two different fractions can name the same part of a whole. These are called **equivalent** fractions.

EXAMPLE

The fractions $\frac{1}{2}$ and $\frac{2}{4}$ name the same part of a whole.

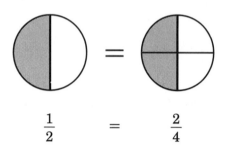

$$\frac{1}{2} \quad = \quad \frac{2}{4}$$

PRACTICE

Directions: Write an equivalent fraction to describe the shaded part of each figure in Numbers 1 and 2.

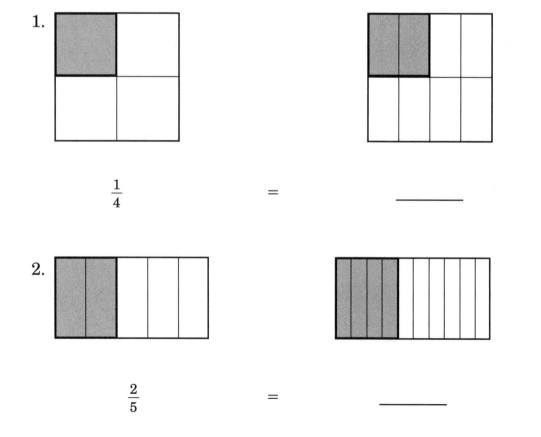

1.

$$\frac{1}{4} \qquad = \qquad \rule{3cm}{0.4pt}$$

2.

$$\frac{2}{5} \qquad = \qquad \rule{3cm}{0.4pt}$$

Directions: Use the following figure to answer Numbers 3 and 4.

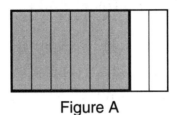

Figure A

3. Write the fraction for the shaded part of Figure A. _____

4. Which of the following figures shows a fraction that is equivalent to the fraction of the shaded part of Figure A?

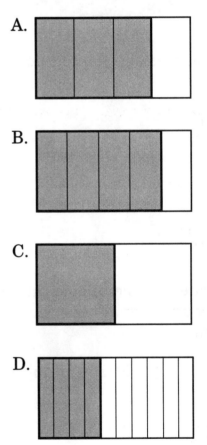

A.

B.

C.

D.

Mixed Numbers

A **mixed number** has a whole number and a fractional part.

EXAMPLE

This much pie was left after the school picnic. How many pies were left?

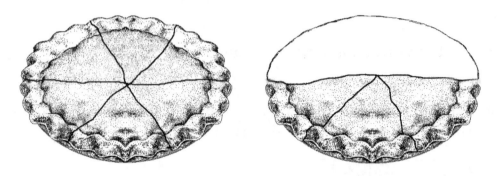

There is 1 whole pie left. The second pie was sliced into 6 equal pieces, and there are 3 pieces left.

$$\textbf{whole number} \rightarrow 1\tfrac{3}{6} \leftarrow \textbf{fraction}$$

There were $1\tfrac{3}{6}$ pies left.

PRACTICE

Directions: For Numbers 1 and 2, write a whole number in the first column and a fraction in the second column. Then write your mixed number in the third column.

Whole number	Fraction	Mixed number
1. _____	_____	_____
2. _____	_____	_____

Directions: Write a mixed number to name the shaded parts of the figures in Numbers 3 through 5.

3.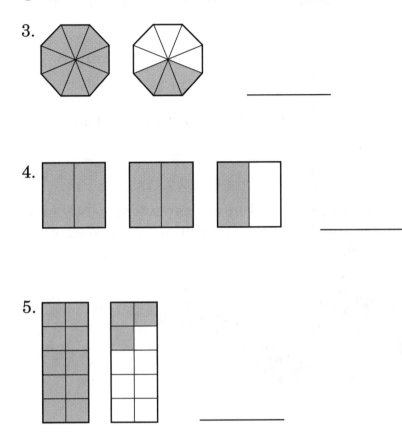

_____

4. _____

5. _____

6. Which mixed number names the shaded parts of the figures?

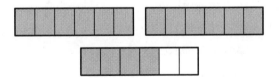

A. $2\frac{2}{4}$

B. $2\frac{4}{6}$

C. $1\frac{8}{3}$

D. 3

Comparing and Ordering Fractions

When comparing and ordering fractions, first look at the denominator.

$$\text{denominator} \rightarrow \frac{1}{2} \qquad\qquad \frac{1}{10} \leftarrow \text{denominator}$$

The smaller the denominator, the bigger the piece or part is (when numerators are equal).

EXAMPLE

The candy bar on the left is divided into 2 parts. The candy bar on the right is divided into 10 parts. Look at one part of each candy bar. Then compare the size of the two parts.

$\frac{1}{2}$ is bigger than $\frac{1}{10}$.

By using symbols, you can write the following:

$$\frac{1}{2} > \frac{1}{10} \qquad\qquad \text{or} \qquad\qquad \frac{1}{10} < \frac{1}{2}$$

TIP: Think of it this way: If you were only going to get one part of something you like, would you rather choose from 2 large equal parts or 10 small equal parts?

PRACTICE

Directions: For Numbers 1 through 4, write > or < on the lines.

1. $\frac{1}{4}$ ———— $\frac{1}{3}$ $\frac{1}{3}$ ———— $\frac{1}{4}$

2. $\frac{1}{2}$ ———— $\frac{1}{6}$ $\frac{1}{6}$ ———— $\frac{1}{2}$

3.

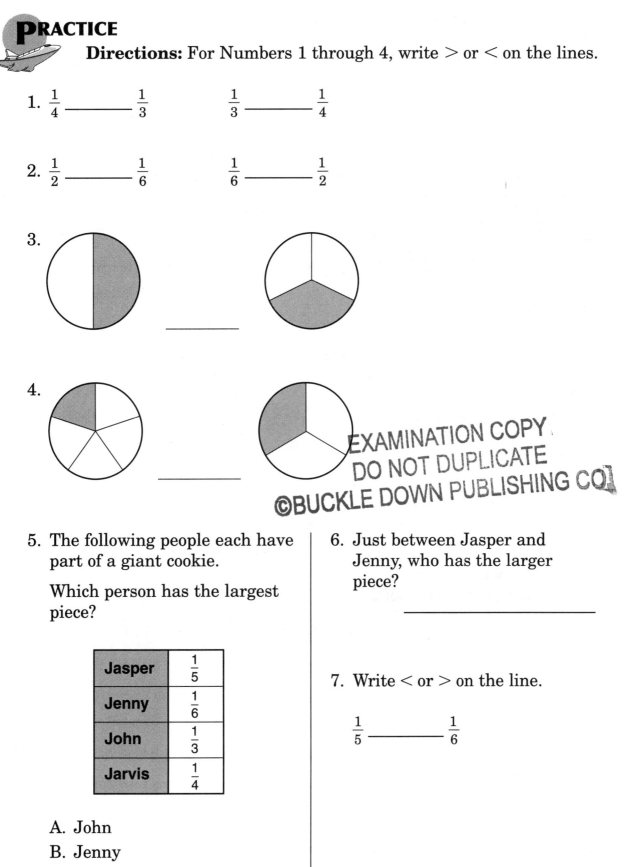

4.

5. The following people each have part of a giant cookie.

   Which person has the largest piece?

Jasper	$\frac{1}{5}$
Jenny	$\frac{1}{6}$
John	$\frac{1}{3}$
Jarvis	$\frac{1}{4}$

   A. John
   B. Jenny
   C. Jarvis
   D. Jasper

6. Just between Jasper and Jenny, who has the larger piece?

   ————————————————

7. Write < or > on the line.

   $\frac{1}{5}$ ———— $\frac{1}{6}$

TEST YOUR SKILLS

Directions: This pizza has pepperoni on part of it. Use it to answer Numbers 1 and 2.

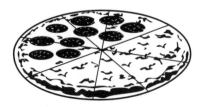

1. What fraction names the part of the pizza with pepperoni?

    A. $\frac{1}{8}$

    B. $\frac{2}{8}$

    C. $\frac{3}{8}$

    D. $\frac{4}{8}$

2. What fraction names the part of the pizza without pepperoni?

    A. $\frac{1}{2}$

    B. $\frac{1}{3}$

    C. $\frac{1}{4}$

    D. $\frac{1}{5}$

Directions: Use the pictures to answer Numbers 3 and 4.

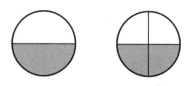

3. Which fractions name the shaded parts?

    A. $\frac{1}{2}$ and $\frac{2}{4}$

    B. $\frac{1}{2}$ and $\frac{1}{4}$

    C. $\frac{1}{2}$ and 1

    D. $\frac{1}{4}$ and $\frac{2}{4}$

4. Which of the following correctly compares the shaded parts?

    A. $\frac{1}{2} > \frac{2}{4}$

    B. $\frac{1}{2} < \frac{2}{4}$

    C. $\frac{1}{2} + \frac{2}{4}$

    D. $\frac{1}{2} = \frac{2}{4}$

Directions: Use the pictures to answer Numbers 5 through 7.

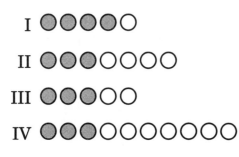

5. Which picture shows $\frac{3}{5}$ of the circles shaded?

    A. I
    B. II
    C. III
    D. IV

6. Which picture shows more than $\frac{3}{5}$ of the circles shaded?

    A. I
    B. II
    C. III
    D. IV

7. Which picture shows $\frac{4}{7}$ of the circles **not** shaded?

    A. I
    B. II
    C. III
    D. IV

Directions: Use the circles to answer Numbers 8 and 9.

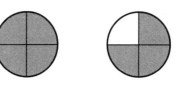

8. Which mixed number names the shaded parts of the circles?

    A. $1\frac{1}{4}$

    B. $1\frac{2}{4}$

    C. $1\frac{3}{4}$

    D. $1\frac{3}{8}$

9. Which of the following is correct?

    A. $1\frac{1}{4} > 1\frac{2}{4}$

    B. $1\frac{2}{4} < 1\frac{3}{4}$

    C. $1\frac{3}{4} = 1\frac{3}{8}$

    D. $1\frac{3}{8} < 1\frac{1}{4}$

10. Which shows the fractions in order from **least** to **greatest**?

    A. $\frac{2}{7}, \frac{2}{3}, \frac{2}{5}$

    B. $\frac{2}{7}, \frac{2}{5}, \frac{2}{3}$

    C. $\frac{2}{3}, \frac{2}{5}, \frac{2}{7}$

    D. $\frac{2}{5}, \frac{2}{7}, \frac{2}{3}$

11. Which drawing shows $1\frac{5}{6}$ of the figures shaded?

    A.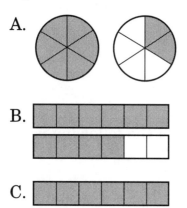

    B.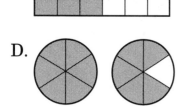

    C.

    D.

12. Felicia answered 9 questions on a test correctly. There were 10 questions on the test. What is the fraction that names the part of the test that Felicia answered correctly?

    A. $\frac{1}{9}$

    B. $\frac{1}{10}$

    C. $\frac{9}{10}$

    D. $\frac{10}{9}$

13. Which of the following figures shows a fraction that is equivalent to the shaded part of this figure?

    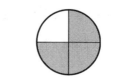

    A.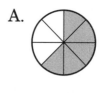

    B.

    C.

    D.

Lesson 3

Computation and Number Properties

When you compute with numbers, you make new numbers from a set of old numbers. The new numbers are related to the ones you started with. Number properties are rules that help us understand and work with numbers. When it's time to work with numbers, remember that calculators can be cool, but your brain is your most important tool.

Addition

When you want to find how many of something there are altogether, you **add (+)**. The numbers that you add are called **addends**. The answer when you add is called the **sum**.

EXAMPLE

Yesterday, Heather received 7 stars for completing her work. Today, she received 3 more. How many stars has Heather received in the last two days?

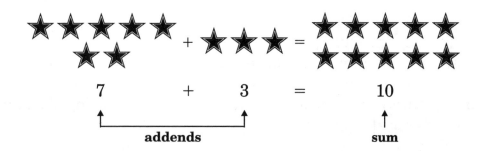

$7 + 3 = 10$ is an **addition number sentence**.

Heather has received 10 stars in the last two days.

When you add numbers, remember that you sometimes need to regroup.

regroup the thousands digit → 1   1 ← **regroup the tens digit**
$$
\begin{array}{r}
3,426 \\
+\ 2,638 \\
\hline
6,064
\end{array}
$$

The sum of 3,426 and 2,638 is 6,064.

PRACTICE

1. Draw a picture that shows 5 + 6.

2. Rodney had 17 baseball cards. His friend David gave him 18 more. How many cards does Rodney now have altogether?

   _____

3. During the summer, 265 different kinds of birds live at the wildlife park. During the winter, another 25 kinds of birds live there. How many different kinds of birds live at the park during the summer and winter altogether?

   _____

4. Add: 4,375 + 5,173 = _____

5. There are 365 days in a common year. How many days are in two common years?

   A. 630
   B. 720
   C. 730
   D. 732

Directions: For Numbers 6 through 8, use the following information.

The third-grade classes had a contest to see which class could collect the most cans for the recycling drive. The table shows how many cans each class collected.

Cans Collected by Students in the Third Grade

Class	Mrs. Johnson	Ms. Santiago	Mr. Potter
Cans Collected	578	717	632

6. What was the total number of cans collected by Mrs. Johnson's and Ms. Santiago's classes combined?

   A. 1,285
   B. 1,295
   C. 1,385
   D. 1,395

7. What was the total number of cans collected by Ms. Santiago's and Mr. Potter's classes combined?

   A. 1,349
   B. 1,359
   C. 1,449
   D. 1,459

8. What was the total number of cans collected by all of the third grade?

   A. 1,707
   B. 1,817
   C. 1,827
   D. 1,927

Subtraction

When you want to take away, find the number left over, or find how many more of something there is, you **subtract (−)**. The answer when you subtract is called the **difference**.

EXAMPLE

This morning, there were 8 hats on the rack in the store. Today, 5 have been sold. How many hats are left on the rack?

$8 - 5 = 3$
↑
difference

$8 - 5 = 3$ is a **subtraction number sentence**.

There are 3 hats left on the rack.

When subtracting numbers, remember that you sometimes need to borrow and regroup.

$$\begin{array}{r} \text{borrow the hundreds digit} \rightarrow 2\ 11 \leftarrow \text{regroup the tens digit} \\ \cancel{3}\cancel{1}9 \\ -\ 198 \\ \hline 121 \end{array}$$

The difference of 319 and 198 is 121.

PRACTICE

1. Draw a picture that shows 9 − 3.

2. Circle the picture that shows 17 − 6.

3. Subtract: 974 − 581 = _____

4. Tommy's wagon can carry 50 pounds. He has some toys in his wagon that weigh 34 pounds. How many more pounds of toys can Tommy's wagon carry?

    A. 16

    B. 26

    C. 74

    D. 84

5. There were 17 birds in a tree above a river. Eight of them flew away. How many are left?

A. 6

B. 7

C. 8

D. 9

6. This table shows the total number of acres in two groves.

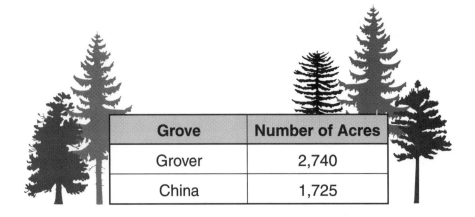

Grove	Number of Acres
Grover	2,740
China	1,725

How many more acres does Grover Grove have than China Grove?

A.   995

B. 1,000

C. 1,015

D. 1,025

7. Which picture shows 7 − 3?

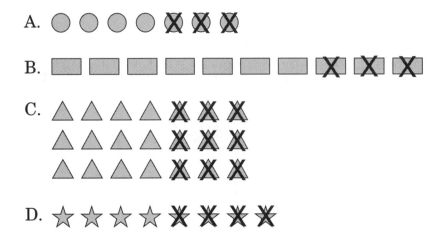

Multiplication

When you want to find how many of an equal number of something there are altogether, you **multiply (×)**. Multiplication is a fast way to do skip counting or repeated addition. The numbers that you multiply are called **factors**. The answer when you multiply is called the **product**.

EXAMPLE

How many slices of bread did it take to make these 3 peanut butter and jelly sandwiches?

There are 2 slices of bread in each sandwich. There are 3 sandwiches.

You can solve this problem using **skip counting**. Skip count by the number of slices from each sandwich.

2, 4, 6

You can also solve it using **repeated addition**. Add the number of slices from each sandwich.

2 + 2 + 2 = 6

This is how you would solve it using multiplication.

2	×	3	=	6
↑		↑		↑
slices in each sandwich		number of sandwiches		total slices of bread

2 × 3 = 6 is a **multiplication number sentence**. The factors are 2 and 3. The product is 6.

It took 6 slices of bread to make 3 peanut butter and jelly sandwiches.

When you multiply numbers, remember that you sometimes need to regroup.

$$1 \leftarrow \textbf{regroup the hundreds digit}$$

$$
\begin{array}{r}
2{,}364 \\
\times \quad 2 \\
\hline
4{,}728
\end{array}
$$

The product of 2,364 and 2 is 4,728.

PRACTICE

1. Multiply: $2{,}143 \times 3 =$ _____

2. Multiply: $635 \times 6 =$ _____

3. Complete the table to show how many slices of bread it takes to make different numbers of sandwiches. There are 2 slices of bread in each sandwich.

Number of Sandwiches	1	2	3	4	5	6	7	8
Slices of Bread	2							

How many slices will it take to make 10 sandwiches? _____

4. Katie puts 4 cookies on each plate. She has 3 plates. How many cookies does she have? Write a multiplication number sentence.

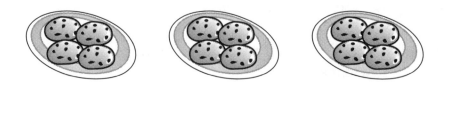

_____ $\times$ _____ $=$ _____

Directions: For Numbers 5 through 7, use the following sets of pears.

5. Use skip counting to find the total number of pears.

_____, _____, _____, _____

6. Use repeated addition to find the total number of pears.

_____ + _____ + _____ + _____ = _____

7. Use multiplication to find the total number of pears.

_____ × _____ = _____

8. Which multiplication number sentence represents the total number of peas?

A. $5 \times 8 = 40$
B. $5 \times 7 = 35$
C. $6 \times 6 = 36$
D. $6 \times 8 = 48$

Multiplication tables

A good way to remember your multiplication facts is to make a table.

PRACTICE

Directions: Fill in the following multiplication table. To get you started, some of the spaces have been filled in for you.

×	1	2	3	4	5	6	7	8	9	10
1										
2			6							
3										
4										
5	5									
6							42			
7										
8										
9				36						90
10										

TIP: If you know your multiplication facts through 10 × 10, you can solve any multiplication problem with whole numbers.

Division

When you break down a number or set of things, you **divide (÷)**. Division is a fast way of doing grouping, repeated subtraction, or equal sharing. The number you are dividing is the **dividend**. The number you are dividing by is the **divisor**. The answer when you divide is the **quotient**. If there is something left over, that number is the **remainder**.

EXAMPLE

Yesterday, the Frozen Treats Ice Cream Shop sold 12 sundaes. A quart of ice cream makes 4 sundaes. How many quarts of ice cream did the Frozen Treats Ice Cream Shop use yesterday to make sundaes?

A quart of ice cream makes 4 sundaes. There were 12 sundaes that were made.

You can solve this problem using **grouping**. A quart of ice cream makes 4 sundaes. Group the 12 sundaes into groups of 4.

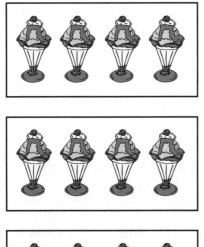

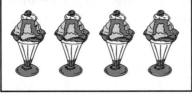

There are 3 groups of 4 sundaes.

The Frozen Treats Ice Cream Shop used 3 quarts of ice cream to make sundaes.

You can also solve this problem using **repeated subtraction**. Start with the number of sundaes that were sold, then subtract the number of sundaes that each quart of ice cream makes. Repeat the subtraction until you can't subtract anymore. Count the number of times you subtracted.

$12 - 4 = 8$ (1 time)

$8 - 4 = 4$ (2 times)

$4 - 4 = 0$ (3 times)

You subtracted 4 from 12 a total of 3 times.

This is how you would solve it using division.

12	÷	4	=	3
↑		↑		↑
number of sundaes		sundaes for each quart		number of quarts

$12 \div 4 = 3$ is a **division number sentence**. The dividend is 12. The divisor is 4. The quotient is 3. There is no remainder.

The Frozen Treats Ice Cream Shop used 3 quarts of ice cream to make sundaes.

 EXAMPLE

Kim and Sue picked 10 flowers. They want to share the flowers equally. How many flowers will each girl get?

You need to **share equally** the 10 flowers. Give one flower to Kim and one to Sue. Repeat until there are no flowers left over.

Kim   Sue   Kim   Sue   Kim   Sue   Kim   Sue   Kim   Sue

Each girl will get 5 flowers. ($10 \div 2 = 5$)

When you divide numbers, remember to keep the right digits lined up.

$$
\begin{array}{r}
18 \leftarrow \textbf{quotient} \\
\textbf{divisor} \rightarrow 6\overline{)108} \leftarrow \textbf{dividend} \\
-\ 6\downarrow \\
\hline
48 \\
-\ 48 \\
\hline
0 \leftarrow \textbf{remainder}
\end{array}
$$

The quotient of 108 and 6 is 18.

PRACTICE

1. Divide: 40 ÷ 5 = _____

2. Divide: 624 ÷ 2 = _____

3. There are 8 friends riding the cars at the amusement park. There are 2 friends in each car.

   How many cars are needed for all 8 friends? _____

4. Jane's dad has an orchard of 160 trees. They are in 8 equal rows. How many trees are in each row?

   A. 17
   B. 18
   C. 19
   D. 20

5. Sammy has 15 marbles. He wants to divide them into 3 equal groups. How many marbles will there be in each group? Use equal sharing by writing the group number (1, 2, or 3) under each marble.

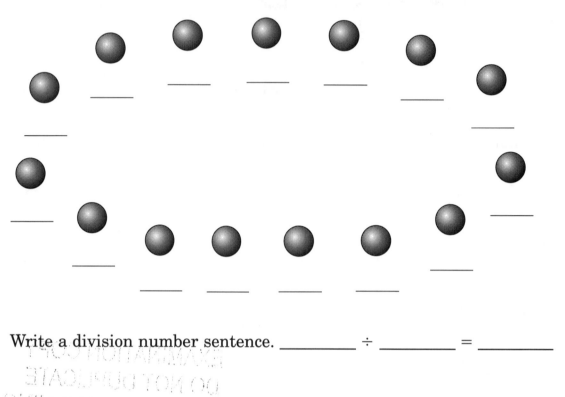

Write a division number sentence. _____ ÷ _____ = _____

6. There are 30 students in Mr. Cody's class. There are 6 students sitting at each table in Mr. Cody's classroom. At how many tables in Mr. Cody's classroom are students sitting? Use repeated subtraction in the space below to solve.

Write a division number sentence. _____ ÷ _____ = _____

Relating multiplication and division

Multiplication and division are "opposites." Multiply any two numbers. Then take the product and divide it by one of the numbers. The quotient will be the other number.

EXAMPLE

Write a multiplication and division number sentence for the following.

multiplication number sentence

$5 \times 3 = 15$

division number sentence

$15 \div 5 = 3$

PRACTICE

Directions: For Numbers 1 and 2, write a multiplication and division number sentence for each.

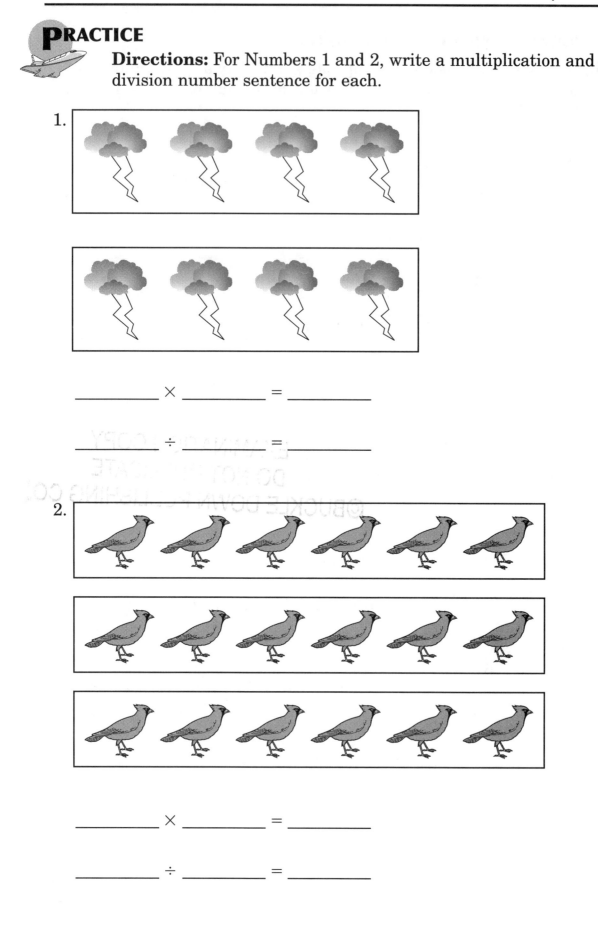

1.

_____ × _____ = _____

_____ ÷ _____ = _____

2.

_____ × _____ = _____

_____ ÷ _____ = _____

Whole Number Properties

Number properties are rules that help us understand and work with numbers.

Identity property for addition

This rule says that when you **add 0** to a number, **the sum** will be equal to that same number.

$$0 + 5 = 5 \qquad\qquad 26 + 0 = 26$$

Commutative property for addition

This rule says that the **order** in which we add numbers **does not change the sum**.

This drawing shows 4 + 2.

There are 6 horses altogether.

What happens when we change the order of the horses?

This drawing shows 2 + 4.

Once again, there are 6 horses altogether.

PRACTICE

1. Color the first 3 squares blue.

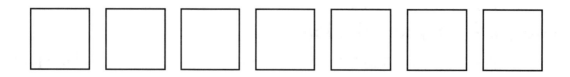

   Now fill in the following blanks.

   _____ blue squares + _____ white squares = 7 squares

   Use the numbers from the blanks to write two different addition number sentences.

   _____ + _____ = 7

   _____ + _____ = 7

Directions: For Numbers 2 through 6, fill in the missing numbers.

2. 10 + _____ = 10

3. 15 + 0 = _____

4. 7 + _____ = 6 + 7

5. 5 + 8 = 8 + _____

6. 13 + _____ = 13

Identity property for multiplication

This rule says that when you **multiply a number by 1**, the product is that **same number**.

$$6 \times 1 = 6 \qquad\qquad 1 \times 10 = 10$$

$$1 \times 6 = 6 \qquad\qquad 10 \times 1 = 10$$

Commutative property for multiplication

This rule says that the **order** of the **factors** (numbers to be multiplied) **does not change the product** (answer).

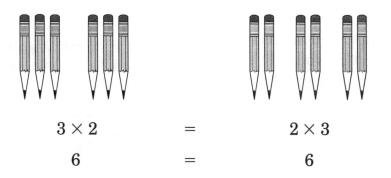

$$3 \times 2 \qquad = \qquad 2 \times 3$$

$$6 \qquad = \qquad 6$$

 **PRACTICE**

1. Use the commutative property for multiplication.

   4×2 is the same as _____ $\times$ _____ .

2. Write two different multiplication sentences using the same two factors of 14.

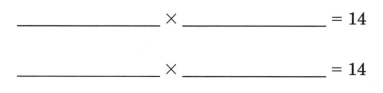

   _____ $\times$ _____ = 14

   _____ $\times$ _____ = 14

Directions: In Numbers 3 through 6, tell whether these real-life situations are like the commutative property. (The results are the same.) Circle your answer.

3. First you eat 3 chocolate cookies, then you brush your teeth; first you brush your teeth, then you eat 3 chocolate cookies.

   Yes   No

4. First you put on your socks, then you put on your shoes; first you put on your shoes, then you put on your socks.

   Yes   No

5. First you pour your cereal in a bowl, then you pour in milk; first you pour in milk, then you pour in cereal.

   Yes   No

6. First you pump up your bike tire, then you put on your helmet; first you put on your helmet, then you pump up your bike tire.

   Yes   No

7. The following number sentence shows the commutative property for multiplication.

   $$4 \times 3 = 3 \times 4$$

   This drawing shows the left-hand side of the number sentence.

   Which drawing shows the right-hand side of the number sentence?

   A.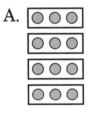

   B.

   C.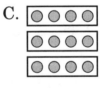

   D.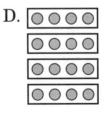

TEST YOUR SKILLS

1. Multiply: 2,435
          × 2

   A. 4,860
   B. 4,870
   C. 4,880
   D. 4,890

2. Which number will make the sentence true?

   $9 \times 3 = ? \times 9$

   A. 1
   B. 3
   C. 5
   D. 15

3. Which number sentence is shown in this picture?

   △△△△△△XXX

   A. $9 + 3 = 12$
   B. $9 - 4 = 5$
   C. $9 - 6 = 3$
   D. $9 - 3 = 6$

4. Subtract: $750 - 687 = ?$

   A. 63
   B. 68
   C. 163
   D. 165

5. Add: 119
       + 87

   A. 106
   B. 172
   C. 196
   D. 206

6. What multiplication number sentence does this picture show?

   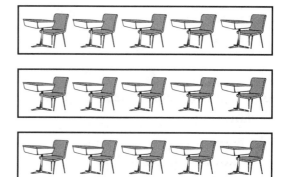

   A. $5 \times 3 = 15$
   B. $6 \times 5 = 30$
   C. $7 \times 4 = 28$
   D. $7 \times 5 = 35$

7. Divide: $20 \div 4 = ?$

   A. 5
   B. 6
   C. 12
   D. 16

8. Each car needs 4 tires. You have 36 tires. On how many cars can you put all 4 tires?

   A. 8
   B. 9
   C. 32
   D. 40

9. Tina has 54 pictures to put in a photo album. If each page holds 6 pictures, how many pages can she fill?

   A. 6
   B. 9
   C. 12
   D. 15

10. Which number belongs inside the box?

    $$\boxed{} \times 15 = 15$$

    A. 1
    B. 3
    C. 5
    D. 15

11. Which of these is an example of the commutative property for multiplication?

    A. $6 + 0 = 6$
    B. $5 \times 1 = 5$
    C. $4 \times 3 = 3 \times 4$
    D. $7 + 8 = 8 + 7$

12. What is another way to write 7×3?

    A. 3×4
    B. 3×5
    C. 3×6
    D. 3×7

13. Can you find the secret number? Here are some clues.

    You can find it when you count by fives.

    The sum of its two digits is 8.

    It is an odd number.

    A. 25
    B. 26
    C. 35
    D. 80

14. Tim had 42 baseball cards. He traded 6 of his cards to Colin for 14 of Colin's cards. How many cards does Tim now have?

    A. 22
    B. 34
    C. 50
    D. 62

Lesson 4

Problem Solving

This step-by-step method will help you solve word problems.

Step 1: **Understand the problem.** What is the problem asking? Find the information needed.

Step 2: **Make a plan.** Choose the correct way to solve the problem.

Step 3: **Solve the problem.** Do the math with the correct operation.

Step 4: **Check your answer.** Use the "opposite" operation to check. In Lesson 3, you saw that multiplication and division are "opposites." Addition and subtraction are also "opposites."

EXAMPLE

Use the step-by-step method to solve this problem.

Phillip's dad had to get 4 new tires put on his car. He paid $264 for the 4 tires. How much did each tire cost?

Step 1: **Understand the problem.**

What is the problem asking?

The cost of each tire.

What information is given in the problem?

4 tires cost $264.

Step 2: **Make a plan.**

What is the correct operation needed to solve the problem?

To find the cost of each tire given the cost of 4 tires, you need to use division.

Step 3: **Solve the problem.**

What is $264 divided by 4?

$$
\begin{array}{r}
66 \\
4\overline{)264} \\
-\ 24\!\downarrow \\
\hline
24 \\
-\ 24 \\
\hline
0
\end{array}
$$

Each tire costs $66.

Step 4: **Check your answer.**

Multiplication is the "opposite" of division. To check a division problem, use multiplication.

$66 \times 4 = 264$

The answer of $66 is correct.

PRACTICE

Directions: Use the following information to answer Numbers 1 through 5.

Colleen has a roll of film that can take 24 pictures. She has already taken 13 pictures. How many more pictures are left to take?

Step 1: **Understand the problem.**

1. What is the problem asking?

   _____

2. What information is given in the problem?

   _____

   _____

Step 2: **Make a plan.**

3. What is the correct operation needed to solve the problem?

  A. addition
  B. subtraction
  C. multiplication
  D. division

Step 3: **Solve the problem.**

4. Write a number sentence and solve the problem. Show your work in the space provided below.

Step 4: **Check your answer.**

5. Show a way to check the math in your answer.

_____

Sometimes it's helpful to write a sentence to answer the question in the problem.

There are _____ more pictures left to take.

↑
fill in your
answer here

Not Enough Information

You **cannot** solve a problem if you do not have all the information.

PRACTICE

Directions: Use the following information to answer Numbers 1 through 3.

Justin bought a baseball bat for $12 and a hat for $3. He also bought a baseball glove. How much did he spend altogether?

Step 1: **Understand the problem.**

1. What is the problem asking?

    _____

2. What information is given in the problem?

    _____

    _____

3. What other piece of information do you need before you can solve the problem?

    _____

When you know there isn't enough information, you don't need to go on to Steps 2, 3, and 4.

Too Much Information

When problems have **extra** information, you can still solve them.

PRACTICE

Directions: Use the following information to answer Numbers 1 through 7.

Marty read 10 pages last night. She read 5 more pages this morning. She read for 30 minutes. How many pages did she read altogether?

Step 1: **Understand the problem.**

1. What is the problem asking?

   _____

2. What information is given in the problem?

   _____

   _____

3. What information is given that is not necessary to solve the problem?

   _____

Step 2: **Make a plan.**

4. What is the correct operation needed to solve the problem?

   A. addition
   B. subtraction
   C. multiplication
   D. division

Step 3: **Solve the problem.**

    5. Write a number sentence and solve the problem.

_____

Step 4: **Check your answer.**

    6. Show a way to check the math in your answer.

_____

    7. Marty read a total of _____ pages.

Problem-Solving Strategies

Not all problems can be solved in the same way. Listed below are some other strategies (or ways) you might use to solve different kinds of problems.

- Write a number sentence.
- Use estimation.
- Make tables, charts, or lists.
- Draw a picture.
- Guess and check.
- Use a calculator.

Now you will see examples of some of these strategies.

Write a number sentence

Number sentences show relationships among numbers.

$$2 + 5 = 7 \qquad\qquad 7 - 3 = 4$$

$$3 \times 3 = 9 \qquad\qquad 15 \div 5 = 3$$

A number sentence does not have any words in it.

PRACTICE

Directions: Write a number sentence and use it to solve the problems for Numbers 1 through 5.

1. Joan put 5 books on her desk. Peter put 6 more books on Joan's desk. How many books are there on Joan's desk?

2. Mr. Allison gave 3 apples to each of his neighbors. He has 7 neighbors. How many apples did Mr. Allison give to his neighbors?

3. Liz had 75 cents. She spent 55 cents on candy. How much does she have left?

4. There are 18 students in Ms. Perez's class. She wants to divide the class into 3 equal groups. How many students will be in each group?

5. Corrine has 10 pieces of candy. Her friend Janet has 2 times as many. How many pieces of candy does Janet have?

Estimation

An **estimate** is an answer that is close but not exact.

Johnny is **about** 4 feet tall.

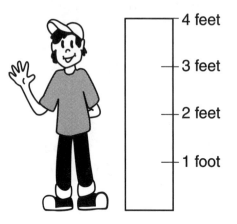

Rounding is a quick way to estimate.

You can round to the nearest **ten:** 10, 20, 30, 40, 50, 60, 70, 80, 90, and so on.

You can round to the nearest **hundred:** 100, 200, 300, 400, 500, 600, 700, 800, 900, and so on.

This comic book costs about 50 cents.

EXAMPLE

The distance between Bedrock and Rock Falls is 69 miles. What is this distance rounded to the nearest 10?

Look at this number line. 69 is closer to 70 than to 60.

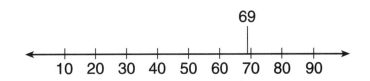

The distance is about 70 miles.

When you are rounding to the nearest 10, follow these rules:

1. If the **digit in the ones place is 5 or greater, round up.**

   45 rounded to the nearest ten is 50.

   78 rounded to the nearest ten is 80.

2. If the **digit in the ones place is less than 5, round down.**

   34 rounded to the nearest ten is 30.

   83 rounded to the nearest ten is 80.

When you are rounding to the nearest 100, follow these rules:

1. If the **digit in the tens place is 5 or greater, round up.**

   156 rounded to the nearest hundred is 200.

   481 rounded to the nearest hundred is 500.

2. If the **digit in the tens place is less than 5, round down.**

   127 rounded to the nearest hundred is 100.

   739 rounded to the nearest hundred is 700.

PRACTICE

1. Round each number to the nearest 10.

   58 _____   41 _____   147 _____

2. Round each number to the nearest 100.

   279 _____   984 _____   123 _____

Make tables, charts, or lists

You can use addition, subtraction, multiplication, or division to help you figure out patterns from tables, charts, or lists. Patterns are covered in greater detail in Lesson 13.

PRACTICE

Directions: For Numbers 1 through 4, follow the pattern to complete the table and answer the question.

1. Every time Emily adds 5 rocks to her rock collection, her dad gives her 3 from his collection. If she collects 35 rocks, how many rocks will her dad have given to her?

   _____

Emily's Rocks	5	10	15	20	25	30	35
Rocks from Dad	3	6					

2. Antonio collects baseball cards. He can buy 6 baseball cards for $2. How much will Antonio spend if he buys 24 cards?

   _____

Number of Cards	6	12	18	24
Cost of Cards	$2	$4		

3. How much will Antonio spend if he buys 30 cards? _____

4. Tammy made a table about spiders and their legs. Help her find the total number of legs that 6 spiders have.

Number of Spiders	1	2	3	4	5	6
Number of Legs	8	16				

   How many total legs do 6 spiders have? _____

Draw a picture

Pictures can be helpful when you need to put things in order.

EXAMPLE

Four students are in line waiting for the bus. Angel is ahead of Winnie. Leslie is between Winnie and Eric. Eric is last in line. In what order are the students in line?

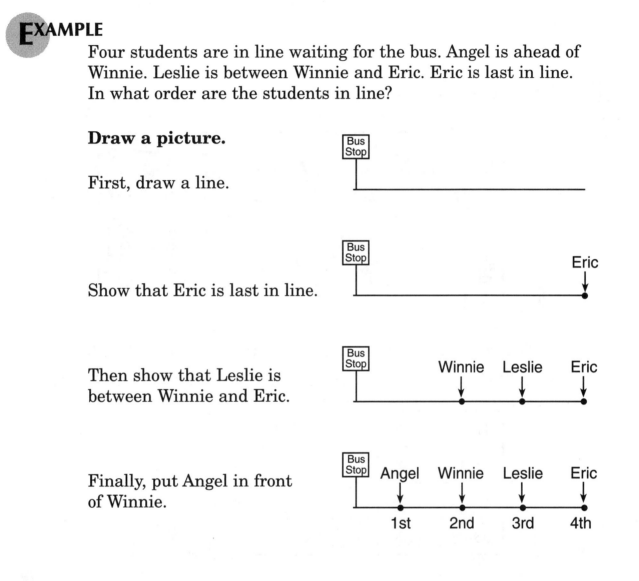

Draw a picture.

First, draw a line.

Show that Eric is last in line.

Then show that Leslie is between Winnie and Eric.

Finally, put Angel in front of Winnie.

PRACTICE

Directions: Draw a picture to solve this problem.

Four students are lined up from shortest to tallest. Arlene is taller than Jeffrey. Diana is shorter than Jeffrey. Mary is taller than Arlene.

shortest   tallest

Who is the tallest? _____

Guess and check

If nothing else seems to be working for you, you can guess and check to see if your answer is correct.

EXAMPLE

Walter bought two things from the school store. He spent 61¢. What two things did he buy?

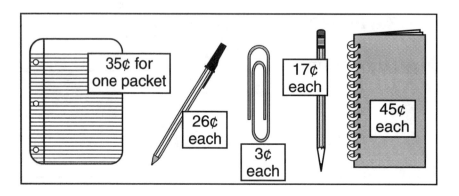

You are looking for two things that will add up to 61¢. Make a table to record your guesses.

17	+	35	=	52¢	Too little
35	+	45	=	80¢	Too much
17	+	26	=	43¢	Too little
35	+	26	=	61¢	Just right

Walter bought a packet of paper and a pen from the school store.

 **TIP:** You can use rounding to help you guess.

Use a calculator

Calculators are great, but if you don't enter the right numbers and operations into the machine, you won't get the right answer!

The drawing below shows the parts of a simple calculator.

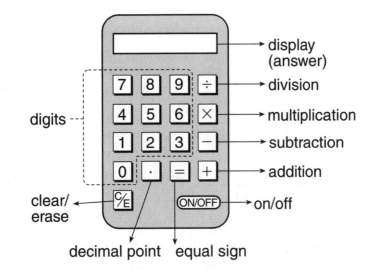

Your teacher asked you to solve this problem: 124 + 625

What do you need to do?

You need to press each digit of the number 124. 1 2 4

Now press the addition key. +

Then press each digit of the number 625. 6 2 5

Press the equal sign. =

The display will show the answer. 749

When working with a calculator remember to . . .

1. press the correct keys.

2. press the equal key = to get an answer.

3. press the clear/erase key ⅌ every time you start a new problem.

PRACTICE

Directions: Choose a strategy and solve each problem for Numbers 1 through 6.

1. Tamika has done 15 push-ups every morning for the last 9 days. How many total push-ups has Tamika done in the last 9 days?

    Tamika has done _____ push-ups in the last 9 days.

2. 432 students have signed up for summer camp. They have been divided into 3 equal groups. How many students are in each group?

    There are _____ students in each group.

3. Rolando bought 3 cans of soup for 99¢. How much does each can of soup cost?

    Each can of soup costs _____ .

4. There are 42 grapes in a bunch. Richard, Theresa, and Gilberto ate all the grapes. They each ate the same number of grapes. How many grapes did Gilberto eat?

Gilberto ate _____ grapes.

5. Jeremy bought 6 bottles of water. Each bottle of water cost $2. How much did Jeremy spend on the 6 bottles of water?

Jeremy spent _____ on the 6 bottles of water.

6. A 6-pack of bottled water sells for $10. How much could Jeremy have saved by buying the 6-pack instead of the 6 separate bottles at $2 each?

Jeremy could have saved _____ buying the 6-pack.

TEST YOUR SKILLS

1. Jerry walks past 16 houses on his way to school. If every house has 1 car parked in the driveway and 1 car parked in the street, how many parked cars will Jerry see when he walks to school?

   Which number sentence would answer this question?

   A. $16 \times 2 = 32$
   B. $16 + 2 = 18$
   C. $16 \times 1 \times 1 = 16$
   D. $16 - 2 = 14$

2. In a race, Frances finished ahead of Marian. Marian finished between Patricia and David. Rick finished ahead of Frances. Who finished first?

   Which of the following strategies would help you answer the question?

   A. make a table
   B. use estimation
   C. draw a picture
   D. write a number sentence

Directions: Use the following information to answer Numbers 3 and 4.

Miss Kristen drives a school bus. One day, she counted a total of 36 boys and girls on the bus.

3. If there were 21 girls, how many boys were there?

   A. 36
   B. 21
   C. 15
   D. 10

4. At the next stop, J.J., Annie, and Flo got on the bus. No one got off the bus. How many children were on the bus after that stop?

   A. 23
   B. 36
   C. 38
   D. 39

5. Bev got an answer of 15. Which of the following problems did she solve?

 A. There are 5 plates on the table. Each plate has 3 sandwiches on it. How many sandwiches are there altogether?

 B. There are 3 baskets of eggs. Each basket has 6 eggs in it. How many eggs are there altogether?

 C. The desks in the room are arranged in rows. There are 4 rows of 5 desks each. How many desks are in the room?

 D. There are 3 chairs. Each chair has 4 legs. What is the total number of legs?

6. The Computer Store sold 4,325 video games in 1999. They sold 5,683 video games in 2000. How many more video games did the Computer Store sell in 2000 than in 1999?

 A. 1,258

 B. 1,358

 C. 1,458

 D. 1,558

7. Raymond has $5. He wants to buy 4 books that cost 96¢ each. Does he have enough money?

 Which of the following strategies will tell him if he has enough money without finding an exact answer?

 A. act it out

 B. draw a picture

 C. make an estimate

 D. write a number sentence

8. Antonio found a special on baseball cards. He can buy 10 cards for $3. How much will 50 cards cost?

Number of Cards	10	20	30	40	50
Cost of Cards	$3	$6	$9		

 A. $12

 B. $15

 C. $18

 D. $30

9. One evening, Tami studied math for 20 minutes. She played outside for 40 minutes. She spent 15 minutes finishing a worksheet for social studies. She read her science book for 10 minutes. That evening, how many minutes did Tami spend on schoolwork?

   What information is given that is **not** necessary to solve the problem?

   A. Tami studied math for 20 minutes.
   B. Tami played outside for 40 minutes.
   C. Tami spent 15 minutes finishing a worksheet for social studies.
   D. Tami read her science book for 10 minutes.

10. Which problem does **not** have enough information given to solve the problem?

   A. Daniel practiced the piano for 30 minutes every day this week. How many minutes did Daniel practice the piano this week?
   B. Julia has collected 35 seashells on her trips to the beach. Craig has collected 28 seashells on his trips to the beach. How many more seashells has Julia collected than Craig on their trips to the beach?
   C. There are 24 students in the third grade. Twelve of the students ride the bus to school. Three students walk to school. The rest ride their bikes to school. How many students ride their bikes to school?
   D. Pat invited six friends to his house for his birthday party. How many hot dogs were eaten at Pat's birthday party?

Spatial Sense, Measurement, and Geometry

The world is filled with objects of all lengths, capacities, and weights. A rain puddle might be 1-foot wide, a swimming pool might hold 12,500 gallons of water, and an elephant might weigh 5,000 kilograms.

There are all kinds of two- and three-dimensional figures in the objects around you. Once you start looking, you will see triangles, circles, rectangles, cubes, cones, spheres, and other figures in the things around you.

In this unit, you will measure and estimate the length, capacity, and weight of objects. You will count coins, estimate cost, and figure out change. You will tell time using both analog and digital clocks. You will measure temperature in both degrees Fahrenheit and degrees Celsius. You will also learn about plane and solid figures, including how to measure perimeter and area.

In This Unit

Length

Capacity

Weight

Money

Time and Temperature

Plane Figures

Solid Figures

Lesson 5

Length

You can measure length (or distance or height) using U.S. customary or metric units. Round your measurements to the nearest unit in this lesson.

U.S. Customary Units of Length

Inches, feet, and yards are some of the U.S. customary units used to measure length.

Inches

An **inch (in.)** is the smallest U.S. customary unit. To measure in inches, use an inch ruler.

EXAMPLE

How many inches long is this fork?

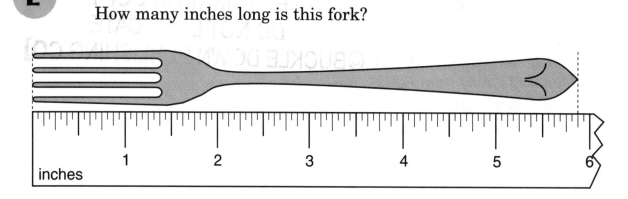

The fork is **about** 6 inches long.

EXAMPLE

Estimate (guess) how far it is from the top of this page to the bottom of this page in inches. Circle your estimate.

about 8 inches   about 11 inches   about 14 inches

Now measure how far it is from the top of this page to the bottom of this page with an inch ruler.

It is about 11 inches from the top of this page to the bottom of this page.

PRACTICE

Directions: For Numbers 1 through 3, estimate the length of each object in inches. Then measure with an inch ruler.

1.

Estimate: about _____ in.

Measurement: _____ in.

2.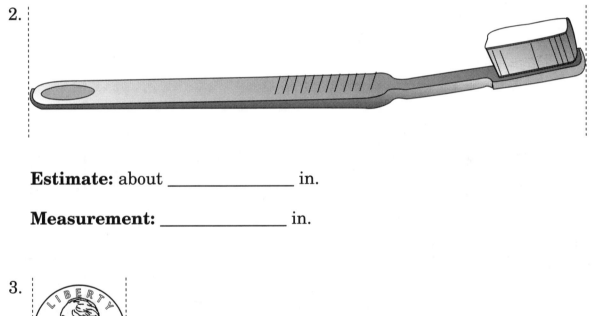

Estimate: about _____ in.

Measurement: _____ in.

3.

Estimate: about _____ in.

Measurement: _____ in.

4. Measure the length of the longer side of your desktop in inches.

   The length of the longer side of your desktop is about _____ in.

   Now measure the length of the shorter side of your desktop in inches.

   The length of the shorter side of your desktop is about _____ in.

5. How wide is the doorway to your classroom in inches?

   The doorway is about _____ inches wide.

6. Measure the length and width of this rectangle in inches.

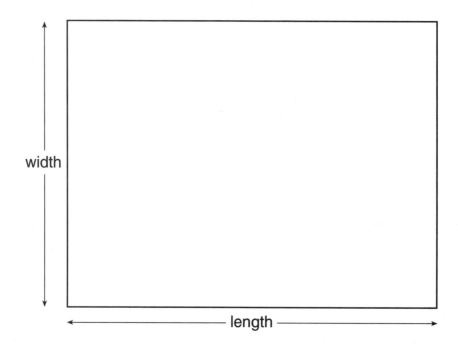

   The length of the rectangle is _____ inches.

   The width of the rectangle is _____ inches.

Feet and yards

Feet (ft) and **yards (yd)** are the U.S. customary units used to measure longer objects or distances.

1 foot = 12 inches

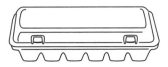

A real-life egg carton is about 1 foot long.

1 yard = 3 feet

The distance from the top of a real-life bench to the ground is about 1 yard.

It is very important to measure using the correct unit. Remember the U.S. customary units of length in order from smallest unit to largest unit are inch, foot, and yard.

EXAMPLE

What U.S. customary unit would you **most likely** use to measure the length of a football field?

Since a football field is really long, you would most likely use **yards** to measure its length.

PRACTICE

1. Estimate the length of your teacher's desk in feet. Then measure the length of your teacher's desk in feet.

   Estimate: about _____ ft

   Measurement: _____ ft

2. Estimate the length of a wall in your classroom in yards. Then measure the length of the wall in yards.

   Estimate: about _____ yd

   Measurement: _____ yd

3. What U.S. customary unit would you **most likely** use to measure the width of your hand?

   _____

4. What U.S. customary unit would you **most likely** use to measure your height?

   _____

5. Name some objects that are about 1 inch in length.

   _____

   _____

6. Name some objects that are about 1 foot in length.

   _____

   _____

7. Name some objects that are about 1 yard in length.

_____

_____

8. Would it take you a **greater** number of inches, feet, or yards to measure the length of a basketball court? Explain your answer.

_____

_____

9. Which is the **best** estimate for the height of a soda can?

   A. 1 yard
   B. 2 feet
   C. 4 yards
   D. 5 inches

10. Which is the **best** estimate for the length of a minivan?

   A. 2 yards
   B. 9 inches
   C. 17 feet
   D. 23 inches

11. Which is the **best** estimate for the width of 1 lane of traffic on an interstate highway?

   A. 2 feet
   B. 4 yards
   C. 18 inches
   D. 22 feet

Metric Units of Length

Centimeters and meters are two metric units used to measure length (or distance or height).

Centimeters

A **centimeter (cm)** is a little less than half as long as an inch. To measure in centimeters, use a centimeter ruler.

XAMPLE

How many centimeters long is this crayon?

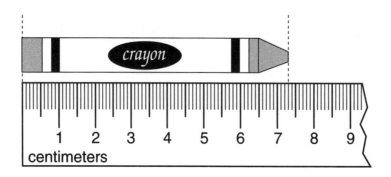

The crayon is **about** 7 centimeters long.

**RACTICE**

Directions: For Numbers 1 through 4, estimate the length of each object in centimeters. Then measure with a centimeter ruler.

1.

Estimate: about _____ cm

Measurement: _____ cm

2.

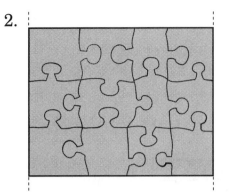

Estimate: about _____ cm

Measurement: _____ cm

3.

Estimate: about _____ cm

Measurement: _____ cm

4. Your height. (Ask a friend to help you.)

Estimate: about _____ cm

Measurement: _____ cm

5. How tall is your desk in centimeters?

My desk is about _____ centimeters tall.

Meters

A **meter (m)** is the metric unit used to measure longer objects or distances. A meter is a little longer than a yard.

1 meter = 100 centimeters

A real-life major league baseball bat is about 1 meter in length.

Since there are 100 centimeters in a meter, a centimeter is a smaller unit than a meter.

EXAMPLE

What metric unit would you **most likely** use to measure the length of a delivery truck?

You would most likely use **meters** to measure the length of a delivery truck.

PRACTICE

1. Estimate the length of your teacher's desk in meters. Then measure the length of your teacher's desk in meters.

   Estimate: about _____ m

   Measurement: _____ m

2. Estimate the length of a wall in your classroom in meters. Then measure the length of the wall in meters.

   Estimate: about _____ m

   Measurement: _____ m

3. What metric unit would you **most likely** use to measure the length of a soccer field?

   _____

4. What metric unit would you **most likely** use to measure the length of your shoe?

   _____

5. Name some objects that are about 1 centimeter in length.

   _____

   _____

6. Name some objects that are about 1 meter in length.

   _____

   _____

7. Would it take you a **smaller** number of centimeters or meters to measure the length of your school building? Explain your answer.

   _____

   _____

8. Which is the **best** estimate for the length of a pen?

   A. 2 meters

   B. 7 centimeters

   C. 12 meters

   D. 15 centimeters

9. Which is the **best** estimate for the height of an elephant?

   A. 3 meters

   B. 9 meters

   C. 13 centimeters

   D. 46 centimeters

TEST YOUR SKILLS

1. Which is the **best** estimate for the distance from the floor to the ceiling in your classroom?

   A. 2 yards
   B. 9 feet
   C. 12 yards
   D. 28 inches

2. Which is the **best** estimate for the length of a pair of scissors?

   A. 15 cm
   B. 15 m
   C. 50 cm
   D. 50 m

3. What is the length of this eraser to the nearest centimeter? Use your ruler to measure.

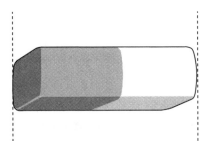

   A. 2 centimeters
   B. 3 centimeters
   C. 4 centimeters
   D. 5 centimeters

Directions: For Numbers 4 and 5, use your ruler to measure the following paper clip.

4. What is the length of the paper clip to the nearest inch?

   A. 1 inch
   B. 2 inches
   C. 3 inches
   D. 4 inches

5. What is the length of the paper clip to the nearest centimeter?

   A. 1 centimeter
   B. 2 centimeters
   C. 3 centimeters
   D. 4 centimeters

6. Which is the **best** estimate for the length of a bed?

   A. 4 yards
   B. 6 feet
   C. 14 inches
   D. 27 inches

Lesson 6

Capacity

When you measure how much liquid you have, you are measuring capacity. Round your measurements to the nearest unit in this lesson.

U.S. Customary Units of Capacity

Cups, pints, quarts, and gallons are some U.S. customary units used to measure capacity.

Cups, pints, quarts, and gallons

Cups (c) are used to measure small amounts of liquid. Use **pints (pt), quarts (qt),** and **gallons (gal)** to measure larger amounts.

1 cup = 8 fluid ounces

1 pint = 2 cups

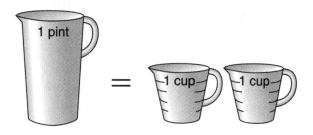

1 quart = 2 pints = 4 cups

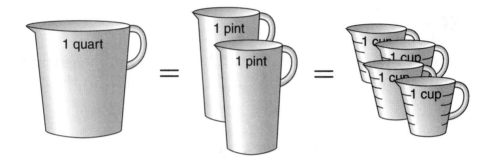

1 gallon = 4 quarts

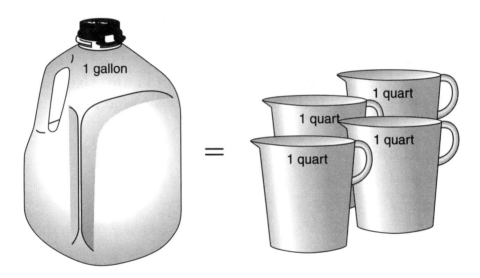

It is very important to measure using the correct unit. Remember, the U.S. customary units of capacity in order from smallest unit to largest unit are cup, pint, quart, and gallon.

 EXAMPLE

What U.S. customary unit would you **most likely** use to measure the capacity of a swimming pool?

You would most likely use **gallons** to measure the capacity of a swimming pool.

PRACTICE

Directions: For Numbers 1 through 6, fill in the table with real-life objects. First estimate the capacities of the objects using U.S. customary units. Then measure their capacities using U.S. customary units. Write in the units you used for your measurement.

	Object	Estimate	Measurement
1.			
2.			
3.			
4.			
5.			
6.			

7. What U.S. customary unit would you **most likely** use to measure the capacity of a coffee mug?

   _____

8. What U.S. customary unit would you **most likely** use to measure the capacity of a kitchen sink?

   _____

9. Name some objects that hold about 1 cup.

_____

_____

10. Name some objects that hold about 1 pint.

_____

_____

11. Name some objects that hold about 1 quart.

_____

_____

12. Name some objects that hold about 1 gallon.

_____

_____

13. Which is the **best** estimate of how much water a drinking glass holds?

   A. 1 qt
   B. 2 c
   C. 3 pt
   D. 4 gal

14. What U.S. customary unit would you **most likely** use to measure the capacity of a large barrel?

   A. cups
   B. pints
   C. quarts
   D. gallons

Metric Units of Capacity

Milliliters and liters are some of the metric units used to measure capacity.

Milliliters

Milliliters (mL) are used to measure small amounts of liquid. A real-life medicine dropper holds about 1 milliliter.

Liters

Liters (L) are used to measure larger amounts of liquid. A liter is a little more than 1 quart.

1 liter = 1,000 milliliters

Since there are 1,000 milliliters in a liter, a milliliter is a smaller unit than a liter.

EXAMPLE

What metric unit would you **most likely** use to measure the capacity of a spoon?

You would most likely use **milliliters** to measure the capacity of a spoon.

PRACTICE

Directions: For Numbers 1 through 6, fill in the table with real-life objects. First estimate the capacities of the objects using metric units. Then measure the capacities using metric units. Write in the units you used for your measurement.

	Object	Estimate	Measurement
1.			
2.			
3.			
4.			
5.			
6.			

7. Which real-life object most likely holds 1 liter? Circle the correct answer.

8. What metric unit would you **most likely** use to measure the capacity of a can of soda?

_____

9. What metric unit would you **most likely** use to measure the capacity of a gas can?

_____

10. Name some objects that hold about 1 milliliter.

_____

_____

11. Name some objects that hold about 1 liter.

_____

_____

12. **About** how many liters of water are in this fish tank?

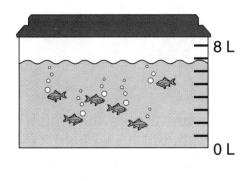

8 L

0 L

A. 5 L

B. 6 L

C. 7 L

D. 8 L

13. Which is the **best** estimate of the capacity of a large bottle of liquid laundry soap?

A. 4 L

B. 40 mL

C. 40 L

D. 400 mL

TEST YOUR SKILLS

1. Which measurement is the **greatest**?

   A. 40 liters of soda

   B. 100 liters of water

   C. 200 milliliters of orange juice

   D. 500 milliliters of seawater

2. Which unit of measurement would you **most likely** use if you were measuring the amount of water in a full bathtub?

   A. cups

   B. quarts

   C. pints

   D. gallons

3. **About** how much liquid is shown in this drinking glass?

   A.   2 milliliters

   B.   20 milliliters

   C.   200 milliliters

   D. 20,000 milliliters

4. Which of these holds the **least** amount of liquid?

   A.  1 cup

   B. 1 quart

   C. 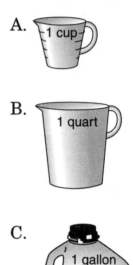 1 gallon

   D.  1 pint

5. A jar has marks showing how much liquid it can hold. One of the marks shows 4 liters. How many milliliters is 4 liters?

   A.   400

   B. 1,000

   C. 2,000

   D. 4,000

Lesson 7

Weight

When you measure how heavy an object is, you are measuring weight. Round your measurements to the nearest unit in this lesson.

U.S. Customary Units of Weight

Ounces and pounds are the U.S. customary units used to measure weight.

Ounces

Ounces (oz) are used to weigh light objects.

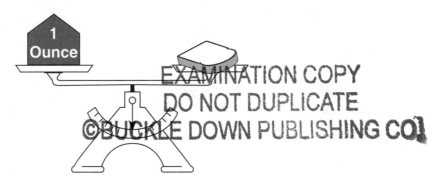

A real-life slice of bread weighs about 1 ounce.

Pounds

Pounds (lb) are used to weigh heavier objects.

1 pound = 16 ounces

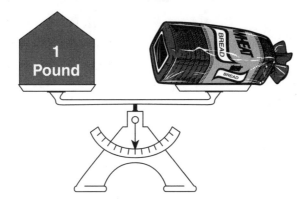

A real-life loaf of bread weighs about 1 pound.

It is very important to measure using the correct unit. Since there are 16 ounces in a pound, an ounce is a smaller unit than a pound.

EXAMPLE

What U.S. customary unit would you **most likely** use to measure the weight of a pine cone?

You would most likely use **ounces** to measure the weight of a pine cone.

PRACTICE

Directions: For Numbers 1 through 6, fill in the table with real-life objects. First estimate the weights of the objects using U.S. customary units. Then measure the weights using U.S. customary units. Write in the units you used for your measurement.

	Object	Estimate	Measurement
1.			
2.			
3.			
4.			
5.			
6.			

7. What U.S. customary unit would you **most likely** use to measure the weight of a bicycle?

   _____

8. What U.S. customary unit would you **most likely** use to measure the weight of a green bean?

   _____

9. Name some objects that weigh about 1 ounce.

   _____

   _____

10. Name some objects that weigh about 1 pound.

    _____

    _____

11. Which is the **best** estimate of the weight of a bag of sugar?

    A. 2 oz
    B. 5 lb
    C. 23 lb
    D. 400 oz

12. Which is the **best** estimate of the weight of a pear?

    A. 6 oz
    B. 8 lb
    C. 10 lb
    D. 35 oz

Metric Units of Weight

Grams and kilograms are two metric units used to measure weight.

Grams

Grams (g) are used to weigh light objects.

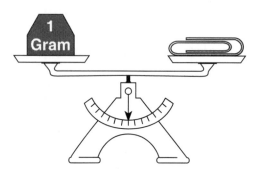

A real-life paper clip weighs about 1 gram.

Kilograms

Kilograms (kg) are used to weigh heavier objects. A kilogram is a little more than 2 pounds.

1 kilogram = 1,000 grams

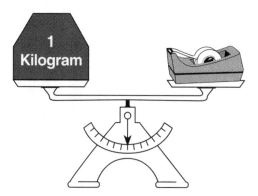

A real-life tape dispenser weighs about 1 kilogram.

Since there are 1,000 grams in a kilogram, a gram is a smaller unit than a kilogram.

EXAMPLE

What metric unit would you **most likely** use to measure the weight of a baby?

You would most likely use **kilograms** to measure the weight of a baby.

PRACTICE

Directions: For Numbers 1 through 6, fill in the table with real-life objects. First estimate the weights of the objects using U.S. customary units. Then measure the weights using U.S. customary units. Write in the units you used for your measurement.

	Object	Estimate	Measurement
1.			
2.			
3.			
4.			
5.			
6.			

7. What metric unit would you **most likely** use to measure the weight of a leaf?

   _____

8. What metric unit would you **most likely** use to measure the weight of a dictionary?

   _____

9. Name some objects that weigh about 1 gram.

   _____

   _____

10. Name some objects that weigh about 1 kilogram.

    _____

    _____

11. Which is the **best** estimate of the weight of a feather?

    A. 1 g
    B. 4 kg
    C. 15 kg
    D. 300 g

12. Which is the **best** estimate of the weight of a horse?

    A. 2 kg
    B. 12 g
    C. 145 g
    D. 450 kg

TEST YOUR SKILLS

1. What is the **best** estimate of the weight of a real-life cat?

   A.   4 kg
   B.   40 kg
   C.   400 kg
   D. 4,000 kg

2. Which of these is the **heaviest**?

   A. 1 kg
   B. 5 g
   C. 8 kg
   D. 1,000 g

3. What is the **best** estimate of the weight of a real-life telephone?

   A. 2 oz
   B. 3 lb
   C. 6 oz
   D. 16 lb

4. What is the **best** estimate of the weight of a bee?

   A. 2 g
   B. 6 kg
   C. 18 kg
   D. 115 g

5. Which of these real-life objects weighs about 1 pound?

   A.

   B.

   C.

   D.

Lesson 8

Money

Knowing how to count money is important in life. The following shows the coins that are most often used, along with their values. It also shows a one-dollar bill.

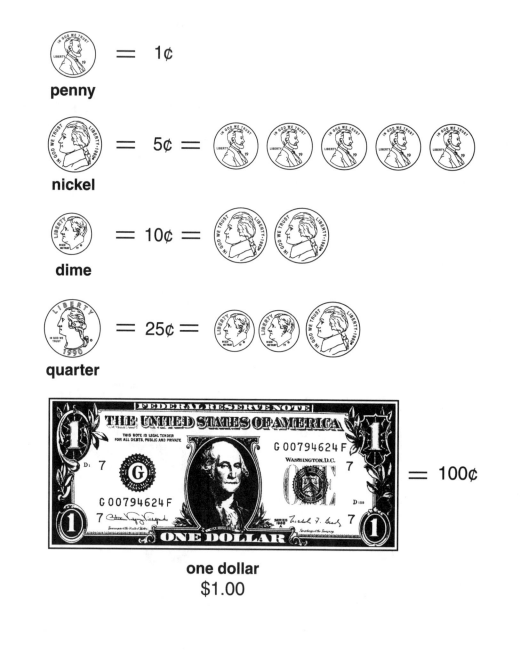

one dollar
$1.00

TIP: Other bills that are used a lot are the five-dollar, the ten-dollar, and the twenty-dollar bill.

We show dollars and cents with symbols and words.

EXAMPLES

$5   or $5.00   five dollars

11¢   or $0.11   eleven cents

$5.11   five dollars and eleven cents

PRACTICE

Directions: For Numbers 1 through 4, circle the correct answer.

1. Three dollars and ten cents is the same as:

   $310 $3.10

2. One hundred fifteen cents is the same as:

   $1.15 $0.15

3. Four dollars is the same as:

   $0.40 $4.00

4. $15.03 is the same as:

   fifteen dollars and thirty cents   fifteen dollars and three cents

5. Which person has the most money?

A. Paula

B. Annette

C. Steve

D. Indira

Directions: For Numbers 6 and 7, write the amount of money that is shown. Then draw the same amount of money a different way. Show the value of each of your coins.

6.

_____

7.

_____

Getting Change

Change is the amount of money you get back when you pay more than is
necessary for something.

EXAMPLE

Chris bought a 25¢ postcard for a friend.

She paid with $1.00. How much change did she get back?

Follow these steps to find out how much change she got back.

Step 1: **Write the numbers so that the decimal points (.) and the
place values are lined up.**

$$\$\ 1\ .\ 0\ 0$$
$$-\ \$\ 0\ .\ 2\ 5$$

Step 2: **Subtract. Borrow and regroup when necessary.**

$$\$\ \overset{0}{\cancel{1}}\ .\ \overset{9}{\cancel{0}}{}^{1}0$$
$$-\ \$\ 0\ .\ 2\ 5$$
$$\overline{\$\ 0\ .\ 7\ 5}$$

Chris got back 75¢ in change.

PRACTICE

Directions: Use the items and prices to answer Numbers 1 through 3.

1. What did José buy with exactly the amount shown below?

_____

2. Robby bought a book. He gave the clerk $2.00. How much change did he get back?

_____

3. Lori bought a box of crayons for 49¢. She gave the clerk $1.00. Which group of coins shows the change she got back?

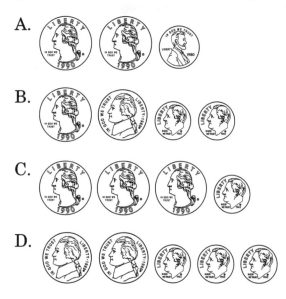

A.

B.

C.

D.

Estimating with Money

Sometimes you estimate to see if you have enough money to buy something.

PRACTICE

Linda has $0.67. She is looking at the chart that shows prices of food.

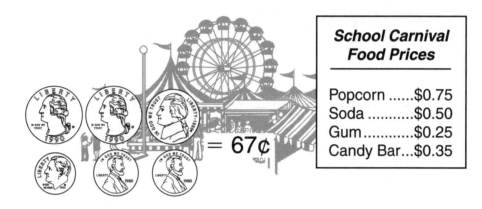

Directions: Circle the answer that tells if she has enough money to buy the item in Numbers 1 through 4.

1. popcorn   Yes   No

2. soda   Yes   No

3. gum   Yes   No

4. candy bar   Yes   No

5. If she wants to buy 2 different items, what 2 items could she buy?

_____

6. If she wanted 1 of each item, how much money would she need altogether?

_____

7. How much more money does Linda need to buy 1 of each item?

_____

You can also estimate how much change you should get back.

EXAMPLE

Alice bought a large box of crayons for $4.95. She gave the clerk $10.00. **About** how much change should she get back?

Estimating the Difference	Finding the **Exact** Difference
$10.00	$10.00
− **5.00**	− 4.95
$5.00	$5.05

Alice should get back about $5.00 in change.

PRACTICE

1. Jake and his mom went to the grocery store. They saw blueberries on sale.

$1.98
per pint

Jake and his mom have $10.00. Can they buy 5 pints of blueberries?

_____

Directions: Use the prices below to answer Numbers 2 through 5.

Marbles
$0.75

Yo-Yo
$1.25

Kite
$2.55

Baseball
$3.00

Rachel has $0.98.

2. Does she have enough money to buy a bag of marbles? _____

3. Does she have enough money to buy a yo-yo? _____

4. What is the **best** estimate of the cost of 2 bags of marbles and a baseball?

   A. $3.00
   B. $5.00
   C. $7.00
   D. $9.00

5. Lorraine bought a kite. She paid for it with a five-dollar bill. What is the **best** estimate of how much change she got back?

   A. $2.50
   B. $2.60
   C. $3.40
   D. $3.50

TEST YOUR SKILLS

Directions: Use the chart to answer Numbers 1 through 4.

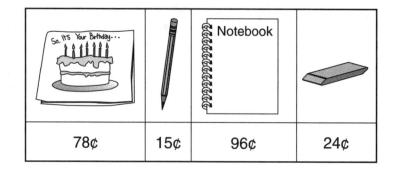

78¢	15¢	96¢	24¢

1. Luke bought an eraser. He gave the clerk $1.00. How much change did he get back?

   A. 30¢
   B. 46¢
   C. 76¢
   D. 84¢

2. Jay paid for an item with one dollar and got back 85¢ in change. What did he buy?

   A. a card
   B. a pencil
   C. an eraser
   D. a notebook

3. Jenny bought a birthday card. She paid with $1.00. Which group of coins shows the change that she got back?

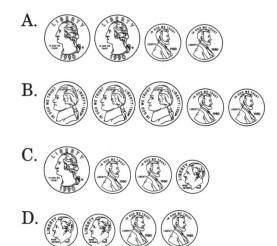

4. Carlos bought a pencil for 15¢. He paid with a quarter. How much change did he get back?

   A. 5¢
   B. 10¢
   C. 15¢
   D. 20¢

Directions: Use the price list to answer Numbers 5 through 8.

Price List

Silver whistle.......$1.67
Rubber ball $0.55
Airplane $1.95
Dump truck $1.35

5. Steve has $0.75.

Which of the items does Steve have enough money to buy?

A. airplane
B. rubber ball
C. dump truck
D. silver whistle

6. If Duncan bought a dump truck and paid for it with a five-dollar bill, how much change did he get back?

A. $3.65
B. $3.55
C. $3.45
D. $3.35

7. Christina wants to buy 2 airplanes. What is the **best** estimate of the cost of 2 airplanes?

A. $2.00
B. $3.00
C. $4.00
D. $0.04

8. If you wanted to buy one of each item, how much money would you need?

A. $5.52
B. $4.17
C. $2.82
D. $2.55

Time and Temperature

Time tells you what part of the day it is or how long it takes an event to occur. Temperature is the measure of how hot or cold something is.

Time

Time is measured using a clock.

This is called a **digital clock**.   This is called an **analog clock**.

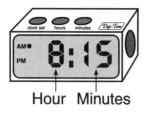

Hour   Minutes

Each day has 24 hours. The 12 hours from midnight to noon are called the A.M. hours. The 12 hours from noon to midnight are called the P.M. hours. A digital clock has a little light beside the time that shows whether it is A.M. or P.M. An analog clock does not show if it is A.M. or P.M.

The short hand of the analog clock points to the hours. The big numbers around the clock show the hours. The long hand points to the minutes. The little marks around the clock show the minutes. There are 5 minutes between each of the big numbers. There are 60 minutes in one hour. This clock shows 8:15.

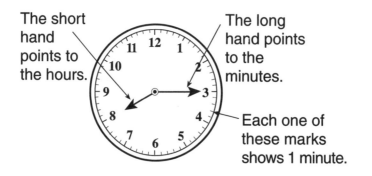

The short hand points to the hours.

The long hand points to the minutes.

Each one of these marks shows 1 minute.

If it is between midnight and noon, it would be 8:15 A.M. If it is between noon and midnight, it would be 8:15 P.M.

Elapsed time

Elapsed time is the amount of time that has passed between two given times.

EXAMPLES

Jamie went outside at 10:35 A.M. She came back inside at 11:15 A.M. How long was she outside?

Since the long hand is pointing to a big number on both clocks, you can skip count by 5's.

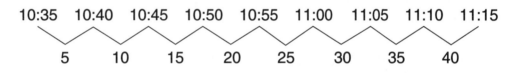

Jamie was outside for 40 minutes.

Frankie gets done with lunch at school at 12:10 P.M. School gets out at 3:20 P.M. How long is it from the end of Frankie's lunch until school gets out?

Count the hours first. Then the minutes.

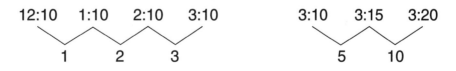

It is 3 hours and 10 minutes from the end of Frankie's lunch until school gets out.

PRACTICE

Directions: For Numbers 1 through 7, write the time shown on the clock. Be sure to include A.M. or P.M.

1. It is between noon and midnight.

_____

2. It is between midnight and noon.

_____

3. It is between noon and midnight.

_____

4.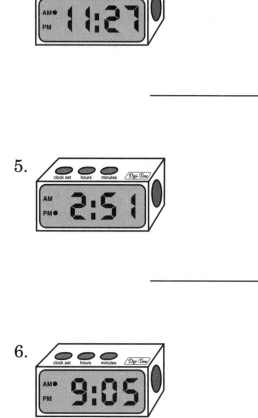

_____

5.

_____

6.

_____

7.

_____

8. It is 5:00 P.M. What time will it be in 3 hours and 15 minutes?

_____

9. Leena's family left their house in Riverdale at 8:00 A.M. to drive to Mount Airy. They arrived in Mount Airy at 1:24 P.M. How long did it take for Leena's family to drive from Riverdale to Mount Airy?

_____

10. On Saturday morning, Michelle played soccer. The clock shows the time she left her house.

She returned home 2 hours and 14 minutes later. Draw the hands on the clock to show the time she returned home. Then write the time on the line.

_____

Temperature

Temperature is measured in degrees using a thermometer. The U.S. customary unit is **degrees Fahrenheit (°F)**. The metric unit is **degrees Celsius (°C)**.

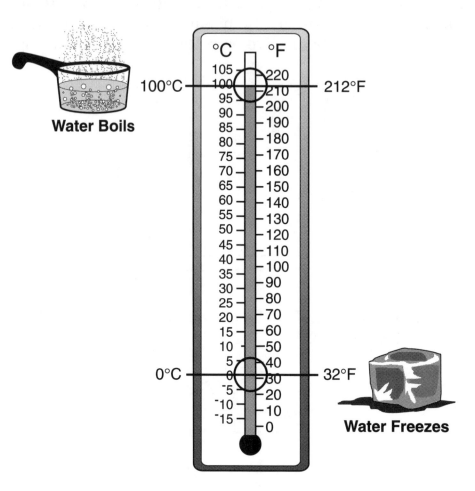

The average temperature in Alaska in January is 5°F or −13°C.

The average temperature in Hawaii in January is 68°F or 20°C.

XAMPLE

What temperature is shown on the following thermometer? Write the temperature in both °F and °C.

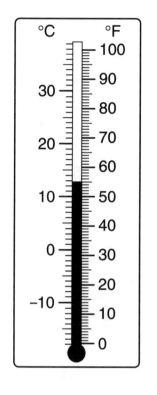

The temperature shown is 55°F or about 13°C.

**RACTICE**

1. Circle the temperature at which you would **most likely** need to wear a jacket.

   40°F   72°F   90°F

2. Steve saw the temperature on a bank thermometer one summer day that read 35°. It was really warm outside. The thermometer was not wrong. How could this be?

Directions: For Numbers 3 through 6, write the temperature shown on each of the thermometers in °F and °C.

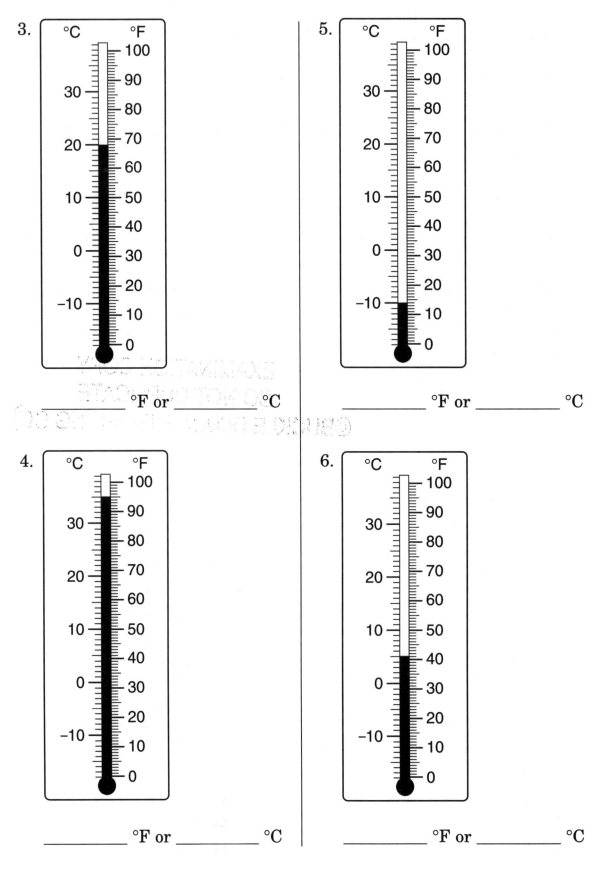

3. _____ °F or _____ °C

5. _____ °F or _____ °C

4. _____ °F or _____ °C

6. _____ °F or _____ °C

7. What are some things you like to do outside when the temperature is 75°F?

_____

_____

8. What are some things you like to do outside when the temperature is 5°C?

_____

_____

9. Which of the following would **most likely** have a temperature shown on this thermometer?

10. Which of the following would **most likely** have a temperature shown on this thermometer?

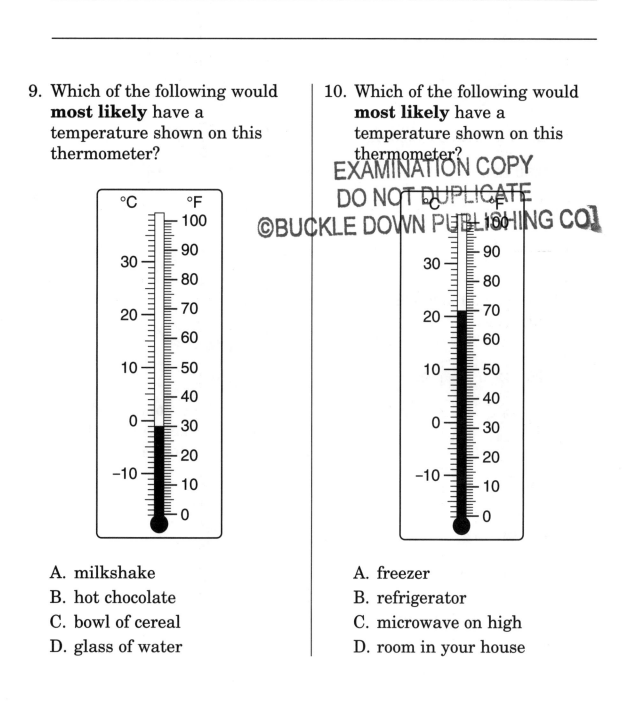

A. milkshake

B. hot chocolate

C. bowl of cereal

D. glass of water

A. freezer

B. refrigerator

C. microwave on high

D. room in your house

TEST YOUR SKILLS

Directions: Use the following information to answer Numbers 1 and 2.

Alec's appointment time is shown on this clock.

1. What time is Alec's appointment?

   A. 3:30 P.M.
   B. 4:15 P.M.
   C. 4:30 P.M.
   D. 4:45 P.M.

2. Alec finished his appointment at this time.

   How long was his appointment?

   A. 45 minutes
   B. 55 minutes
   C. 1 hour and 5 minutes
   D. 1 hour and 15 minutes

3. Which clock shows 11:25?

   A.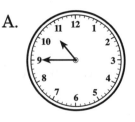

   B.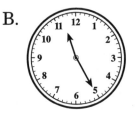

   C.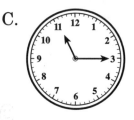

   D.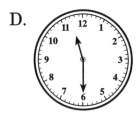

4. On a frozen pond, at about which temperature will the ice **first** start to melt?

   A. 0°F
   B. 11°F
   C. 22°F
   D. 33°F

Directions: Use the following thermometer to answer Numbers 5 and 6.

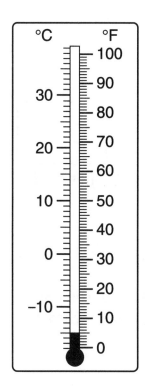

5. What is the temperature in °F?

   A. −15°F

   B. −5°F

   C. 5°F

   D. 15°F

6. What is the temperature in °C?

   A. −15°C

   B. −5°C

   C. 5°C

   D. 15°C

7. Which digital clock shows that 2 hours and 25 minutes have gone by since the time on this clock?

A.

B.

C.

D.

8. One sunny day, Rene looked at the thermometer outside. It read 24°C. Which of these is most likely to be true?

   A. A cup of water left outside will boil.

   B. You will be able to build a snowman.

   C. A cup of water left outside will freeze.

   D. You will be able to play softball outside.

Plane Figures

Shapes such as circles, triangles, and squares are called **plane figures**. They lie on a flat surface. Here are some examples of plane figures:

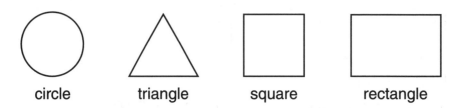

| circle | triangle | square | rectangle |

Polygons

A **polygon** is a closed plane figure made up of 3 or more straight sides. Polygons are named for the number of sides and angles they have.

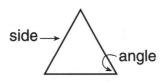

This chart shows you the names of some polygons.

Polygon	Name	Number of Sides and Angles
△	triangle	3
▭	quadrilateral	4
⬠	pentagon	5
⬡	hexagon	6
⯃	octagon	8

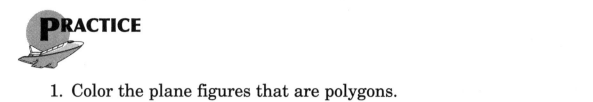

PRACTICE

1. Color the plane figures that are polygons.

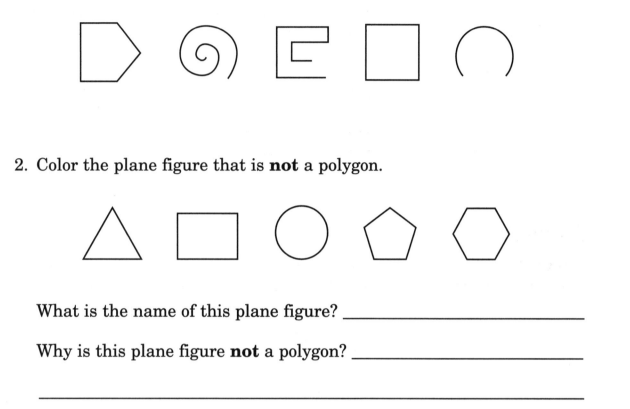

2. Color the plane figure that is **not** a polygon.

What is the name of this plane figure? _____

Why is this plane figure **not** a polygon? _____

_____

3. Draw a line from each real-life object to the polygon it reminds you of.

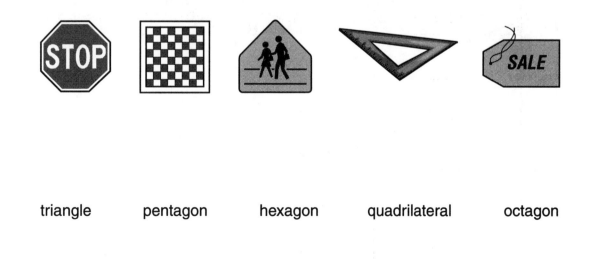

triangle   pentagon   hexagon   quadrilateral   octagon

Directions: For Numbers 4 through 6, write the name of the polygon with the given number of sides and angles.

4. 5 sides and angles _____

5. 3 sides and angles _____

6. 8 sides and angles _____

Directions: For Numbers 7 and 8, draw an example of the given polygon in the space provided.

7. hexagon

8. quadrilateral

9. Which of the following polygons **is not** a triangle?

A.

B.

C.

D.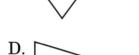

10. Which of the following polygons **is** a quadrilateral?

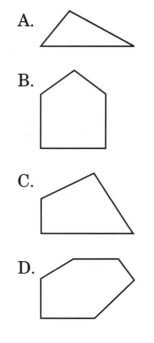

A.

B.

C.

D.

Symmetry

A plane figure has **symmetry** when it can be folded into two parts so that one part fits exactly onto the other. The spot where the plane figure is folded is called the **line of symmetry**. Some plane figures may have more than one line of symmetry.

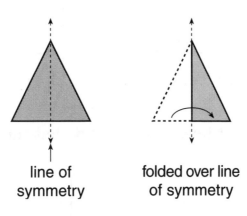

line of
symmetry

folded over line
of symmetry

PRACTICE

1. Which of the following quadrilaterals shows a line of symmetry? Draw a circle around it.

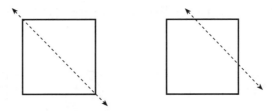

2. Does this plane figure have **more than** one line of symmetry?

_____

3. Which of the following shows a line of symmetry? Trace it with your pencil.

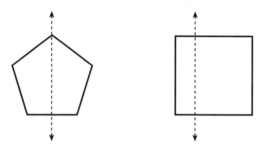

4. Draw all the different lines of symmetry that this square has.

How many lines of symmetry did you draw? _____

5. Which letters **do not** have a line of symmetry? Draw a circle around each one.

  V O **U P**

6. Name some things around you that have at least one line of symmetry.

_____

_____

Congruency

Two or more plane figures are **congruent** when they have the **same shape and size**.

EXAMPLE

Look at the following pairs of plane figures.

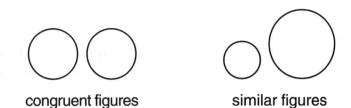

congruent figures   similar figures

The circles on the left are the same size and shape. They are congruent. The circles on the right are the same shape, but are different sizes. They are not congruent.

PRACTICE

1. Circle the pair of plane figures that is congruent.

2. Draw a line to connect all the pairs of figures that are congruent.

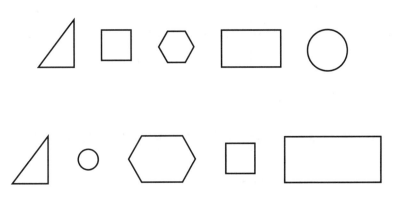

3. Are the hexagons that make up this honeycomb congruent?

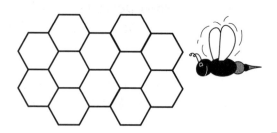

_____

4. Pretend your teacher gave you an octagon and a piece of paper. You have to make an octagon that is congruent to the one your teacher gave you. How would you do it?

_____

_____

5. If you cut this triangle along its line of symmetry, would the two new triangles be congruent?

_____

6. Draw a line that shows where you could cut this square so that the two new plane figures would not be congruent.

7. Name some pairs of things around you that are congruent.

_____

_____

Perimeter

The distance around the outside of a polygon is called the **perimeter**. To find the perimeter of a polygon, **add the lengths of all the sides** of the polygon.

You can measure the lengths of the sides of the figure using standard units of length like inches, feet, yards, centimeters, or meters. Or you can use nonstandard units of length like paper clips, erasers, or anything else you can find. Be sure to label your answer to show what you used for your unit.

EXAMPLE

What is the perimeter of this quadrilateral in centimeters?

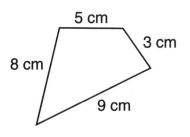

Add the lengths of all the sides of the quadrilateral.

$5 + 3 + 9 + 8 = 25$

The perimeter of the quadrilateral is 25 cm.

EXAMPLE

David used the top of his pencil eraser to measure the lengths of the sides of this triangle. What is the perimeter of this triangle?

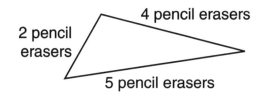

Add the lengths of all the sides of the triangle.

$2 + 4 + 5 = 11$

The perimeter of the triangle is 11 pencil erasers.

PRACTICE

Directions: For Numbers 1 and 2, write the name of an object in your classroom. First estimate the perimeter of the object, then measure its perimeter using a nonstandard unit.

1. object: _____

    Estimate: about _____

    Measurement: _____

2. object: _____

    Estimate: about _____

    Measurement: _____

Directions: For Numbers 3 and 4, find the perimeter of each figure.

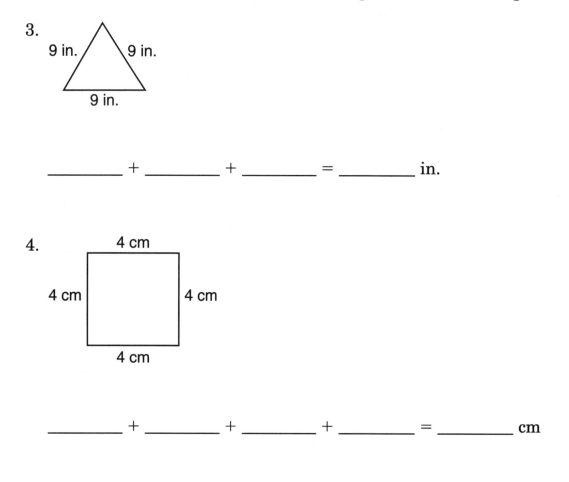

3.

9 in.   9 in.

9 in.

_____ + _____ + _____ = _____ in.

4.

4 cm

4 cm   4 cm

4 cm

_____ + _____ + _____ + _____ = _____ cm

Directions: Use a centimeter ruler to measure the lengths of the sides of the figures in Numbers 5 and 6.

5. Write a number sentence to show how you will add the lengths of the sides.

_____

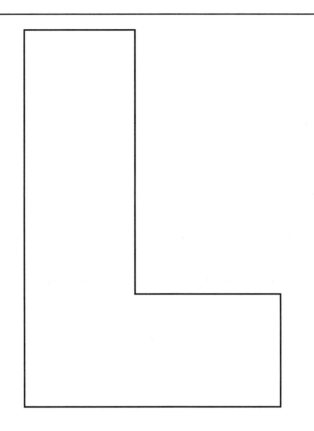

What is the perimeter of this figure? _____

6. Write a number sentence to show how you will add the lengths of the sides.

_____

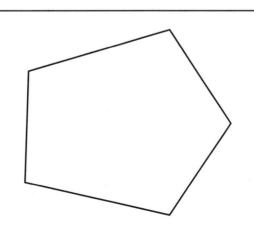

What is the perimeter of this figure? _____

Area

The **area** of a polygon is the number of **square units** needed to cover the surface of the polygon.

The square units you use can be of any size. They may be squares that are 1 inch, 1 foot, 1 yard, 1 centimeter, or 1 meter on a side. Or they can be any other length as long as they are square.

EXAMPLE

What is the area of this square?

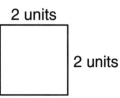

Cover the square with square units to help you find the area.

Each square unit ▦ is 1 unit by 1 unit.

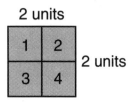

The area of the square is 4 square units.

PRACTICE

Directions: For Numbers 1 and 2, write the name of an object in your classroom. First estimate the area of the object, then measure its area using a square unit that you cut from paper.

1. object: _____

   Estimate: about _____ square units

   Measurement: _____ square units

2. object: _____

   Estimate: about _____ square units

   Measurement: _____ square units

Directions: For Numbers 3 through 6, find the area of each figure in square units.

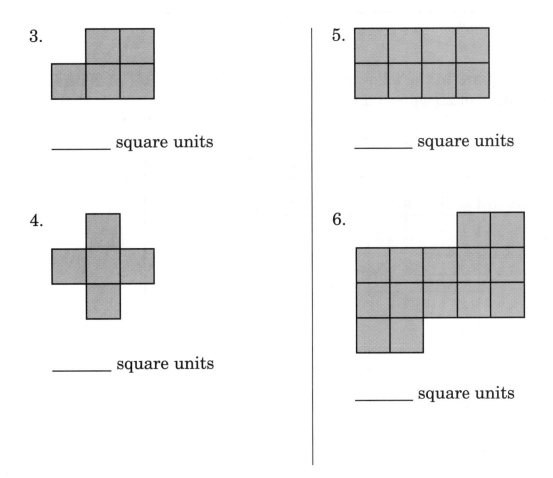

3.

_____ square units

4.

_____ square units

5.

_____ square units

6.

_____ square units

Directions: Use the grids to draw the plane figures in Numbers 7 and 8. Each square in the grid has a length of 1 unit and an area of 1 square unit.

7. Draw a rectangle in the following grid that has a perimeter of 14 units and an area of 12 square units.

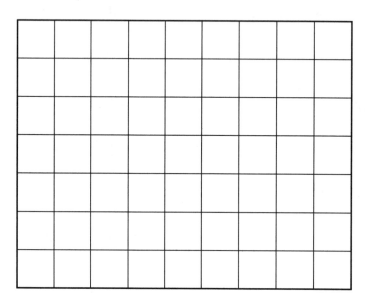

8. Draw a square in the following grid that has a perimeter of 20 units and an area of 25 square units.

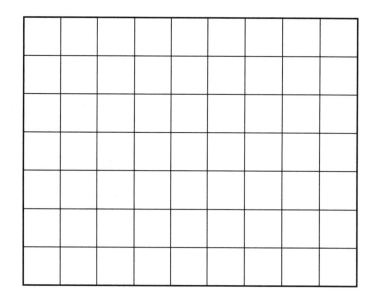

TEST YOUR SKILLS

1. Which of the following plane figures shows a line of symmetry?

   A.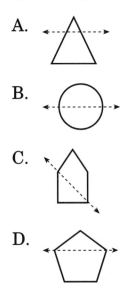

   B.

   C.

   D.

2. How many angles does this plane figure have?

   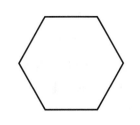

   A. 2
   B. 4
   C. 6
   D. 8

3. Sheila's parents want to put a fence around this vegetable garden. How many meters of fencing will they need?

   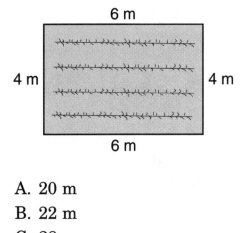

   A. 20 m
   B. 22 m
   C. 28 m
   D. 30 m

4. Which pair of figures is congruent?

   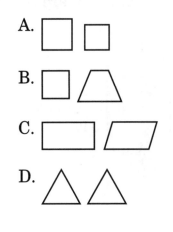

   A.

   B.

   C.

   D.

5. Which of these objects has more than one line of symmetry?

A.

B.

C.

D.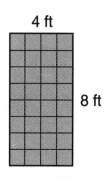

6. The hallway floor to John's bedroom is covered with tiles. Each tile is 1 square foot. What is the area of the hallway floor to John's room in square feet?

4 ft

8 ft

A. 12 square feet
B. 32 square feet
C. 36 square feet
D. 40 square feet

7. Which of these polygons is a pentagon?

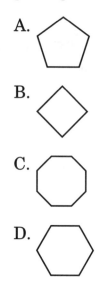

A.

B.

C.

D.

8. The number eight below has two lines of symmetry. One is shown.

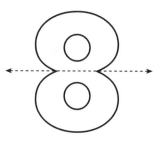

What would the other line of symmetry look like on the drawing?

A.

B.

C.

D.

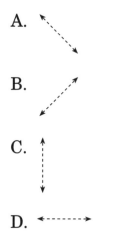

9. A baby dinosaur is searching for his identical twin brother.

Which of these dinosaurs is his twin brother?

A.

B.

C.

D.

10. Which of these polygons has a perimeter of 24 cm?

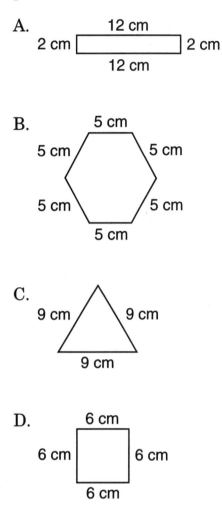

A.
2 cm 12 cm 2 cm
12 cm

B.
5 cm
5 cm   5 cm
5 cm   5 cm
5 cm

C.
9 cm   9 cm
9 cm

D.
6 cm
6 cm   6 cm
6 cm

11. How many sides and angles does an octagon have?

A. 5
B. 6
C. 8
D. 10

Solid Figures

Solid figures are three-dimensional (not flat) shapes. They are sometimes called **space figures**. Some solid figures have **faces**, **edges**, and **vertices**. Other solid figures have **curves**.

vertex – corner point where 3 or more edges meet or the point of a cone

edge – where 2 faces meet

face – plane figure that makes up the solid

Here are some solid figures:

sphere — A **sphere** is a curved solid figure with no faces, no vertices, and no edges.

cone — A **cone** has
1 face
1 vertex
0 edges

cylinder — A **cylinder** has
2 faces
0 vertices
0 edges

cube — A **cube** has
6 faces
8 vertices
12 edges

rectangular prism — A **rectangular prism** has
6 faces
8 vertices
12 edges

square pyramid — A **square pyramid** has
5 faces
5 vertices
8 edges

PRACTICE

Directions: For Numbers 1 through 3, read the sentence. Then write the letters of the figures that match the sentence.

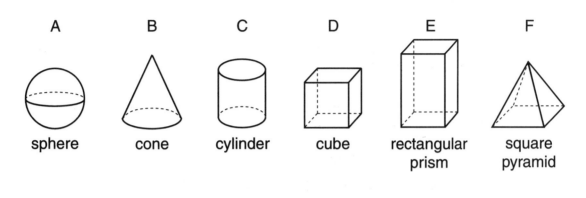

A	B	C	D	E	F
sphere	cone	cylinder	cube	rectangular prism	square pyramid

1. They can roll. _____

2. They have more edges than faces. _____

3. They have no edges. _____

4. Write the name of the solid figure that each object reminds you of.

_____   _____   _____

_____   _____   _____

5. Circle the names of the 2 solid figures that have the same number of faces, edges, and vertices as each other.

   cube   cylinder   cone   rectangular prism   square pyramid

6. Draw a solid figure that has a curved surface.

7. Draw a solid figure that has all flat surfaces.

8. Name objects around you that have the same shape as each of the following solid figures.

   sphere: _____

   cone: _____

   cylinder: _____

   cube: _____

   rectangular prism: _____

   square pyramid: _____

Putting Solid Figures Together

Some real-life objects are made up of different solid figures.

**XAMPLE**

What solid figures make up this baby rattle?

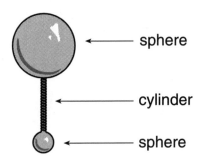

The top and bottom parts of the rattle are spheres and the handle part is a cylinder.

sphere

cylinder

sphere

TIP: Picture taking the real-life objects apart one solid figure at a time to help you see all the solid figures that make up the real-life object.

PRACTICE

Directions: For Numbers 1 through 4, decide which solid figures make up each real-life object. Write the names of the solid figures on the blanks.

1.

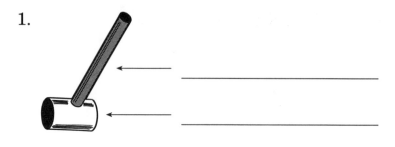

_____

_____

2.

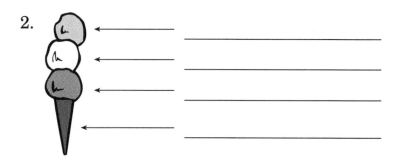

_____

_____

_____

_____

3.

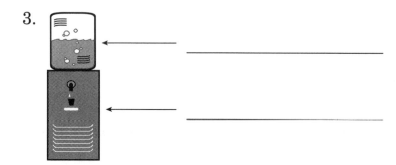

_____

_____

4.

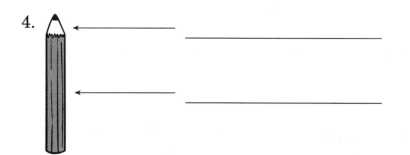

_____

_____

Views of Solid Figures

As you view a solid figure from the top or side you may see plane figures.

EXAMPLE

Think of a party hat that is in the shape of a cone.

What plane figure would you see if you looked at the party hat from the top view?

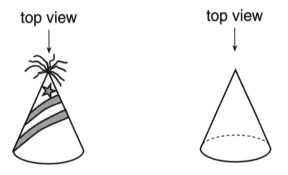

You would see a circle.

What plane figure would you see if you looked at the party hat from the side view?

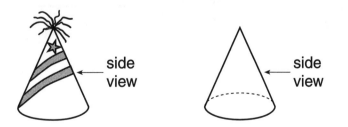

You would see a triangle.

PRACTICE

Directions: For Numbers 1 through 4, write the name of the plane figure you see from both the top and side views.

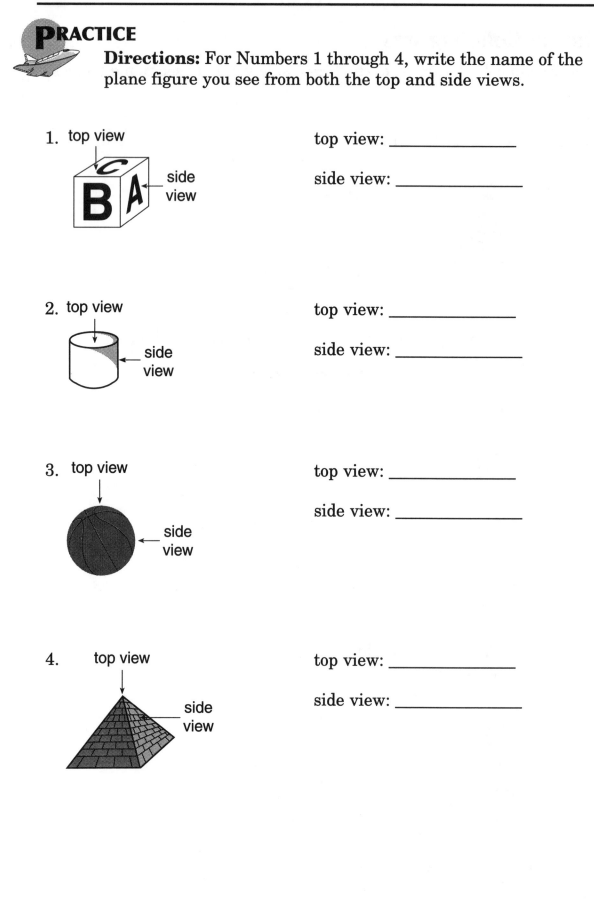

1. top view

    side view

   top view: _____

   side view: _____

2. top view

    side view

   top view: _____

   side view: _____

3. top view

    side view

   top view: _____

   side view: _____

4. top view

    side view

   top view: _____

   side view: _____

Building with Cubes

Cubes can be used to build a three-dimensional figure that looks like a given figure.

 EXAMPLE

Use cubes to build a three-dimensional figure that looks like this one.

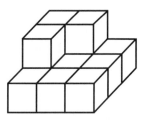

There are 2 levels to this figure. Look at the top level first. It is the easiest one to copy. The top level is made up of 3 cubes that form the letter *L*.

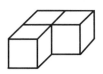

Now look at the bottom level. There are 6 cubes that can be easily seen. In order for the top level to be where it is, there must be cubes under the 3 cubes on the top level. This means that there are 9 cubes on the bottom level. The 3 cubes that are hidden are shown as the shaded cubes below.

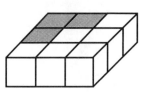

Now put the 2 levels together.

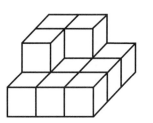

Your figure looks like the one at the top of the page.

PRACTICE

Directions: For Numbers 1 through 6, use cubes to build a three-dimensional figure that looks like the given figure.

1.

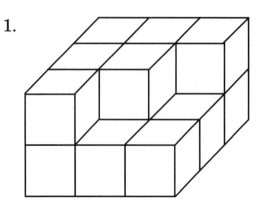

2.

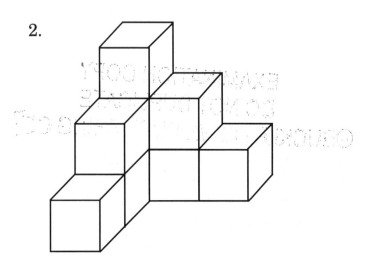

3.

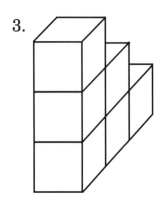

4.

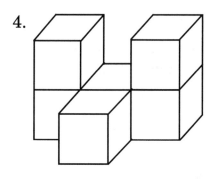

5.

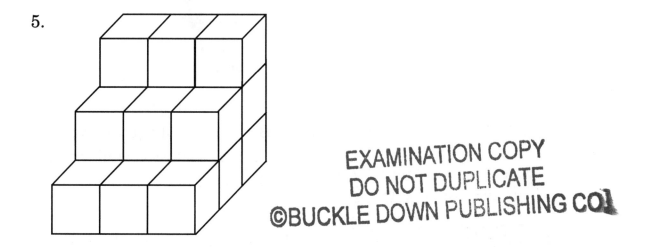

6.

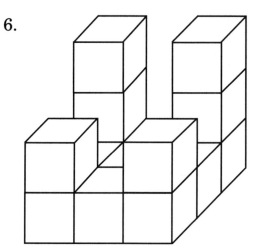

TEST YOUR SKILLS

1. What plane figure are the faces of a cube?

   A.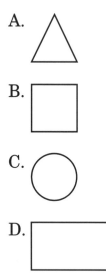

   B.

   C.

   D.

2. Which of these real-life objects most reminds you of a cube?

   A.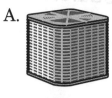

   B.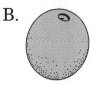

   C.

   D.

3. What two solid figures make up this real-life object?

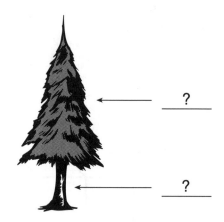

   A. cone and cylinder
   B. sphere and square pyramid
   C. cube and rectangular prism
   D. sphere and rectangular prism

4. Which of these solid figures does **not** have any edges?

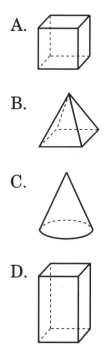

   A.

   B.

   C.

   D.

5. What plane figure would you see from the top view of this dictionary?

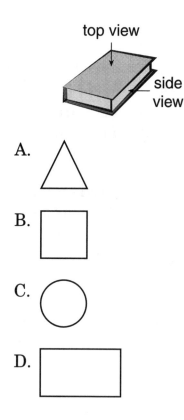

top view

side view

A. △

B. □

C. ○

D. ▭

6. How many vertices does a cone have?

A. 0
B. 1
C. 5
D. 8

7. What do a cone and a cylinder have in common?

A. They have the same number of faces.
B. They have the same number of sides.
C. They have the same number of edges.
D. They have the same number of vertices.

8. Which of these solid figures is a sphere?

A.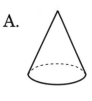

B.

C.

D.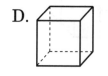

9. What does the bottom level of this three-dimensional figure look like?

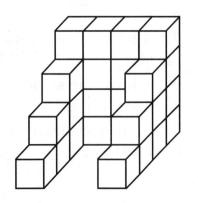

A.
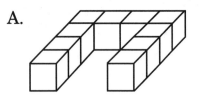

B.
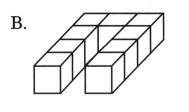

C.
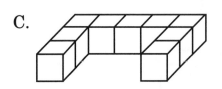

D.
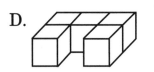

10. What do a cube and a square pyramid have in common?

A. They have curved surfaces.

B. They have 4 faces that are triangles.

C. They have the same number of faces.

D. They have a square face from a bottom view.

11. What plane figure is a face on both a cone and a cylinder?

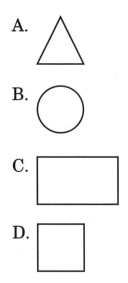

A.

B.

C.

D.

Patterns, Relationships, and Functions

Objects can be grouped based on what they have in common. You may see a robin, a blackbird, and a blue jay at a birdfeeder. Why are different kinds of birds at the same feeder? They have something in common: they eat the same kind of birdseed.

Every Monday morning when you get to school, your teacher gives you a problem to do. What do you expect to happen when you get to school on Monday morning? Your teacher will give you a problem to do. Why do you expect it? Because it's a pattern that has been happening over and over every Monday morning.

In this unit, you will group objects into sets. You will show the relationship of sets by drawing Venn diagrams. You will describe, extend, and analyze number and shape patterns and use them to solve problems.

In This Unit

Relationships

Patterns

143

Lesson 12

Relationships

A **relationship** is how 2 or more objects or ideas are connected to each other. Relationships between individual objects or ideas can be shown by grouping them into sets that have something in common. A picture of the relationships between the sets can be shown in a Venn diagram.

Grouping

You can group objects or ideas in many different ways. They may have the same color, be the same shape, be odd or even numbers, be the same types of food, or have any of a number of other things in common.

EXAMPLE

Patty and Nick were asked to group these objects into sets.

apple, lettuce, corn, banana, lemon, cherry, radish, lime

Patty looked at the objects and noticed that some of the objects were fruits and some were vegetables. She decided to group the objects into 2 sets: fruits and vegetables. Here are her sets.

Fruits: apple, banana, lemon, cherry, lime

Vegetables: lettuce, corn, radish

Nick looked at the objects and noticed that some of the objects were red, some were green, and some were yellow. He decided to group the objects into 3 sets: red objects, green objects, and yellow objects. Here are his sets.

Red Objects: apple, cherry, radish

Green Objects: lettuce, lime

Yellow Objects: corn, banana, lemon

Patty and Nick grouped the same objects in different ways. Both are correct.

PRACTICE

Directions: For Numbers 1 through 4, group the objects into sets. Be sure to label how you grouped the objects.

1. girl, sheep, horse, boy, mom, dog, dad, cat, mouse

_____

_____

2. 2, Y, U, 7, 4, 6, D, 3, R

_____

_____

3. 21, 35, 48, 32, 43, 20, 27, 44, 39

_____

_____

4. January, Thursday, March, October, Monday, Wednesday, May

_____

_____

Directions: For Numbers 5 and 6, write in the labels that show how the objects were grouped into the sets.

5. _____: inch, foot, yard, centimeter, meter

_____: cup, pint, quart, gallon, milliliter, liter

_____: ounce, pound, gram, kilogram

6. _____: beetle, moth, cricket, fly, ant, butterfly

_____: rose, lily, tulip, peony, iris, daisy, marigold

Venn Diagrams

Venn diagrams help you see the relationships between different sets. They show which objects the sets have in common and which objects are in only one set. The objects that are grouped in a set will be within a circle. The label telling how the objects are grouped will be listed in bold face at the top of each circle.

XAMPLE

Here are the Venn diagrams for Patty's and Nick's sets from page 144.

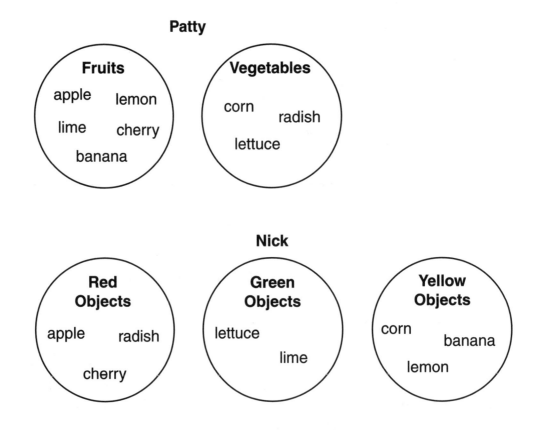

Notice that the circles do not overlap or touch. This means that the sets have no common objects between them.

Sometimes the circles will overlap if there is an object that can be grouped within more than one set. Look at the next example.

EXAMPLE

Jonathon was asked to group these objects into sets.

apple, school bus, corn, banana, lemon, cherry, sun, lime

Jonathon looked at the objects and noticed that some of the objects were fruits and some were objects that are yellow. He decided to group the objects into 2 sets: fruits and yellow objects. Here are his sets.

Fruits: apple, **banana**, **lemon**, cherry, lime

Yellow Objects: school bus, corn, **banana**, **lemon**, sun

Notice that banana and lemon are in both sets. They are both fruits and yellow objects. Here is the Venn diagram to show two sets that have objects in common.

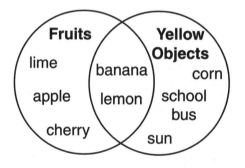

Only the objects that are common to both sets go in the overlapping part of the circles. Notice they are inside each of the circles.

PRACTICE

Directions: For Numbers 1 through 3, draw a Venn diagram to show how the objects were grouped. Be sure to include the labels in your Venn diagram for each set.

1. **Land Animals:** rabbit, fox, sheep, cow, snake, frog, turtle

   Water Animals: shark, eel, sea horse, snake, frog, turtle

2. **Solids:** cube, square pyramid, cone, cylinder, sphere

   Curved Figures: circle, oval, cone, cylinder, sphere

3. **Skip Count by 2's:** 2, 4, 6, 8, 10, 12, 14, 16, 18, 20

   Skip Count by 3's: 3, 6, 9, 12, 15, 18

Directions: For Numbers 4 through 6, use the following Venn diagram.

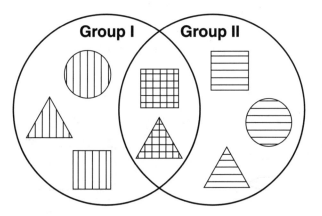

4. Draw all the figures in Group I.

5. Draw all the figures in Group II.

6. Draw all the figures that are common to both Groups I and II.

TEST YOUR SKILLS

1. What was used to group the objects into the following sets?

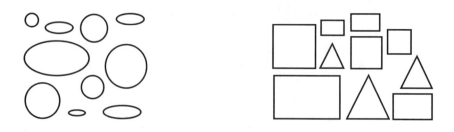

   A. large shapes and small shapes
   B. shapes with 3 sides and shapes with 4 sides
   C. shapes with curves and shapes with straight lines
   D. shapes with big circles and shapes with small circles

2. Creatures from outer space have landed in your schoolyard. At first glance, they all look alike. But look again.

   Which of these best describes how the creatures from outer space can be grouped?

   A. All have 2 arms and 2 legs.
   B. None of them have mouths.
   C. All have 2 feelers and 2 arms.
   D. All have 2 eyes, 2 legs, and 2 feet.

3. Which do the following have in common?

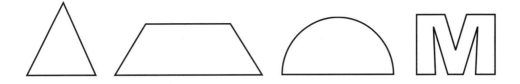

A. They are all polygons.

B. They all have 3 or 4 vertices.

C. They all have only 1 line of symmetry.

D. They all have at least 1 square corner.

Directions: For Numbers 4 and 5, use the following Venn diagram.

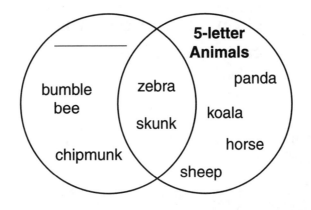

4. Which of these is the label that is missing?

A. Underground Animals

B. Striped Animals

C. Flying Animals

D. Zoo Animals

5. Which of these would be common to both sets?

A. tiger

B. rhino

C. monkey

D. alligator

Patterns

There are different kinds of patterns. Some are number patterns, some are shape patterns, and some use both numbers and shapes. The best way to understand them is to practice working with them.

Number Patterns

Number patterns are based on a **rule**. The rule tells you how to get to the next number in the pattern.

Addition and subtraction number patterns

Addition and subtraction number patterns are formed by adding or subtracting from one number to the next.

EXAMPLES

These train cars show a number pattern. What is the number of the last car?

The rule for the pattern is +5. The number of the last car is 25.

The following tables also show patterns. Here are the rules for going from column A to column B.

Rule: +1

A	B
1 →	2
2 →	3
3 →	4
4 →	5
5 →	6

Rule: −1

A	B
9 →	8
8 →	7
7 →	6
6 →	5
5 →	4

PRACTICE

1. Find the rule for the pattern in the table going from column A to column B.

```
   A      B
  1 ──→  6
  2 ──→  7
  3 ──→  8
  4 ──→  9
  5 ──→ 10
```

Directions: Use the following table to answer Numbers 2 and 3.

```
   A        B
 [  ] ──→  30
  30 ──→  25
  25 ──→  20
  20 ──→ [  ]
  15 ──→ [  ]
```

2. Which number belongs in the empty box in column A?

    A. 10
    B. 15
    C. 25
    D. 35

3. If the number 50 was in column B, what number would be next to it in column A?

    A.   5
    B. 45
    C. 55
    D. 105

Addition number patterns in multiplication

When you do your multiplication facts for a number, a number pattern is formed. Skip counting is a form of multiplication (Lesson 3). When you skip count, you are adding the same number over and over.

XAMPLE

Look at the numbers that are formed when doing your multiplication facts of 9.

$$9 \times 1 = \mathbf{9} \qquad 9 \times 4 = \mathbf{36} \qquad 9 \times 7 = \mathbf{63} \qquad 9 \times 10 = \mathbf{90}$$

$$9 \times 2 = \mathbf{18} \qquad 9 \times 5 = \mathbf{45} \qquad 9 \times 8 = \mathbf{72}$$

$$9 \times 3 = \mathbf{27} \qquad 9 \times 6 = \mathbf{54} \qquad 9 \times 9 = \mathbf{81}$$

Each of the numbers is 9 more than the previous number. The numbers are in a number pattern with the rule +9.

**RACTICE**

1. Look at the number pattern formed by the multiplication facts of 35.

   35, 70, 105, 140, 175, 210

   Use the pattern to find the next three numbers in the multiplication facts of 35.

   _____, _____, _____

2. Look at the number pattern formed by the multiplication facts of 44.

   44, 88, 132, 176, 220, 264

   Use the pattern to find the next three numbers in the multiplication facts of 44.

   _____, _____, _____

3. Look at the number pattern formed when you skip count by 108.

   108, 216, 324, 432, 540, 648

   Use the pattern to find the next three numbers when skip counting by 108.

   _____, _____, _____

Multiplication number patterns

Multiplication number patterns are formed by multiplying from one number to the next.

EXAMPLE

Look at this multiplication number pattern.

3, 9, 27, 81, 243, 729

Each number in the pattern is found by multiplying the number before it by 3.

$3 \times 3 = 9$

$9 \times 3 = 27$

$27 \times 3 = 81$

$81 \times 3 = 243$

$243 \times 3 = 729$

What is the next number in the pattern?

$729 \times 3 = 2{,}187$

The next number in the pattern is 2,187.

PRACTICE

Directions: For Numbers 1 through 4, fill in the blanks to complete each multiplication number pattern.

1. 4, 20, 100, _____, 2,500

2. 2, 4, 8, _____, 32, _____, _____

3. 1, 4, _____, 64, _____

4. _____, 12, 72, 432

Using number patterns to solve problems

Patterns can be used to help you solve problems.

EXAMPLE

A baby giraffe measures 6 feet tall when it is born. If the baby giraffe grows 2 feet every year, how old will it be when it reaches 12 feet tall?

Start with the number 6. Keep adding 2 until your answer is 12. Count how many times you added 2.

$$6 + 2 = 8 \qquad 8 + 2 = 10 \qquad 10 + 2 = 12$$
$$\qquad 1 \qquad\qquad\qquad 2 \qquad\qquad\qquad 3$$

You added 2 three times. The baby giraffe will be 3 years old when it reaches 12 feet tall.

You can also use a **table** to find the answer. Use the same pattern as before. Add 2 feet for each year until the giraffe is 12 feet tall.

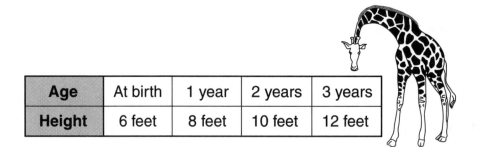

Age	At birth	1 year	2 years	3 years
Height	6 feet	8 feet	10 feet	12 feet

From the table, you can see the giraffe will be 3 years old when it reaches 12 feet tall.

PRACTICE

1. John's mom said she will help him save money. She will put twice the number of pennies in John's piggy bank that he does.

Pennies Put in Piggy Bank

Day	1	2	3	4	5	6	7
John	5	6	7	8	9	10	11
Mom	10	12	14				

How many pennies will John's mom put into his piggy bank on the **seventh** day?

_____

2. What is the rule for the pattern going from John's number of pennies to Mom's number of pennies?

   A. +2
   B. −2
   C. ×2
   D. ÷2

3. Third-graders are filling bags of candy for the school carnival. If the pattern continues, how many bags of candy will the third-graders have filled at 1:00 P.M.? Write your answer in the table.

Time	Number of Bags
9:00 A.M.	30
10:00 A.M.	55
11:00 A.M.	80
12:00 P.M.	105
1:00 P.M.	

4. Write the number that belongs in the empty box in the following table.

2	4	8
6	12	

What is the rule for the pattern if you look in each row (left to right)?

_____

What is the rule for the pattern if you look in each column (top to bottom)?

_____

Directions: Use the following information to answer Numbers 5 and 6.

The United States Mint is making new quarters. Starting in 1999, the mint began making 5 new quarters each year. Each new quarter will have a different state pictured on it. Someday, there will be one quarter for each of the 50 states.

5. Use a number pattern to find how many years it will take before all 50 of the new quarters have been made.

_____

6. In what year will the last 5 quarters be made?

    A. 2002
    B. 2004
    C. 2006
    D. 2008

Shape Patterns

A **shape pattern** repeats circles, squares, triangles, and so on. Order, size, shading, or other markings can also show a pattern.

EXAMPLE

How can you describe this pattern?

There is 1 big triangle, 1 big square, and 1 big circle. Then there is 1 little triangle, 1 little square, and 1 little circle. It looks like the pattern will start over again with 1 big triangle and keep repeating.

What will the next two figures in this pattern be?

The next two figures will be 1 big square and 1 big circle.

Ways to describe shape patterns

1. Look at the **order** of the figures.

2. Look at the **size** of the figures.

3. Look at the **shape** of the figures.

4. Look at the **shading** or **markings** of the figures.

PRACTICE

Directions: For Numbers 1 through 3, fill in the blanks to describe the shape pattern.

1. What is the **order** of the figures? Fill in the rest of the blanks.

circle   square   _____   _____   _____   _____

2. What are the **sizes** of the figures? Fill in the rest of the blanks.

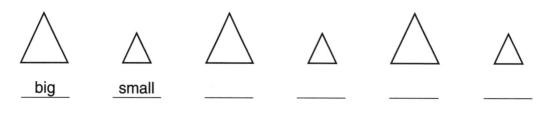

big   small   _____   _____   _____   _____

3. What are the different **shapes** of the figures? Fill in the blanks.

_____   _____   _____   _____   _____   _____

4. Which group of letters shows another way to describe this pattern?

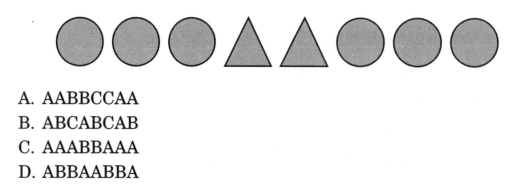

A. AABBCCAA
B. ABCABCAB
C. AAABBAAA
D. ABBAABBA

TEST YOUR SKILLS

Directions: Use the following information to answer Numbers 1 through 4.

Miss Shirley's class likes to play a pattern guessing game.

Miss Shirley wrote this pattern on the chalkboard.

1. What is the rule for the pattern that Miss Shirley wrote?

   A. −5
   B. −6
   C. +5
   D. +6

2. Matt guessed the rule correctly. Now it's his turn.

   He wrote: 30   25   20   ?

   What number comes next in Matt's pattern?

   A. 20
   B. 15
   C. 10
   D. 5

3. Lola guessed Dennis's pattern, then wrote this one on the board:

   What will Lola's next three numbers be?

   A. 50, 55, 60
   B. 55, 65, 75
   C. 60, 70, 80
   D. 50, 60, 70

4. What is the rule for Lola's pattern?

   A. +10
   B. −10
   C. ×10
   D. ÷10

5. Which figure is next in this pattern?

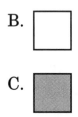

A.

B.

C.

D.

6. What will be next in this pattern?

A. **6**

B. ● ● ●
   ● ● ●

C. △ △ △
   △ △ △

D.

7. Which figure is most likely the next one in this pattern?

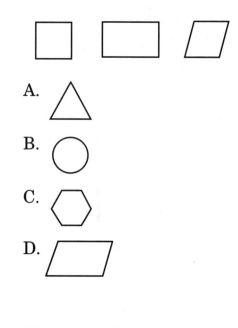

A. △

B. ○

C. ⬡

D. ▱

8. Which number does **not** belong in this pattern?

2, 4, 5, 6, 8, 10, 12

A. 2
B. 5
C. 6
D. 12

9. What is the rule for this pattern?

7, 14, 21, 28, 35, 42

A. ×2
B. ×7
C. +7
D. +14

10. An octopus has 8 arms. Which table shows the correct number of arms for the number of octopuses?

A.

Octopuses	2	3	4	5
Arms	14	22	30	38

B.

Octopuses	2	3	4	5
Arms	15	23	31	39

C.

Octopuses	2	3	4	5
Arms	16	24	32	40

D.

Octopuses	2	3	4	5
Arms	17	25	33	41

11. What is the rule for this pattern?

9, 54, 324, 1,944

A. $+9$

B. $+6$

C. $\times 9$

D. $\times 6$

12. What number comes next in this pattern?

1,221   2,332   3,443   4,554   5,665   _____

A. 5,555

B. 6,556

C. 6,776

D. 7,887

13. Which of these tables shows a pattern going from column A to column B with a rule of +8?

A.

A	B
23	→ 31
29	→ 37
33	→ 41
37	→ 45
44	→ 52

B.

A	B
61	→ 67
62	→ 68
63	→ 69
64	→ 70
65	→ 71

C.

A	B
12	→ 21
24	→ 33
33	→ 42
46	→ 55
50	→ 59

D.

A	B
85	→ 92
87	→ 94
89	→ 96
91	→ 98
93	→ 100

Data, Probability, and Statistics

Have you ever seen a chart or graph in the newspaper or on TV? These are ways that people use to show a lot of information at the same time. Some charts or graphs are used to compare data while others are used to show how things have changed over time.

Have you ever flipped a coin with a friend to see who will go first in a game? This is a fair way to decide because you both have the same chance of winning.

In this unit, you will collect, organize, display, and answer questions about data. You will name the ordered pairs of objects located on grids. You will order events on time lines. You will also describe the probability of an event occurring and list arrangements and combinations of objects.

In This Unit

 **Lesson 14**

Data Collection and Analysis

Data can be collected, organized, and displayed so that it is easy to read and understand. The data can then be used to draw conclusions or make predictions.

Collecting Data

You can **collect data** by doing an experiment.

XAMPLE

> Experiment to see where the spinner stops the most.

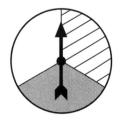

> The spinner was spun 15 times. Here are the results:
>
> > gray, striped, white, white, gray, striped, striped, white, white, gray, striped, gray, striped, gray, gray
>
> Look at the data that was collected. The spinner stopped on the gray area the most number of times.

You can also collect data by asking a question. This is called taking a **survey**.

XAMPLE

> Jimmy asked the other third-graders this survey question: *"What is your favorite lunch?"* Here are the results:
>
> > hot dogs, pizza, spaghetti, soup, pizza, hot dogs, hamburgers, chili, hot dogs, soup, soup, hamburgers, spaghetti, soup, pizza, pizza, hamburgers, pizza, soup, pizza
>
> Look at the data that has been collected. Pizza was the lunch that was answered the most number of times.

Mode

The **mode** in a set of data is the value or result that occurs the most number of times. The value or result must occur more than once. There may be more than one mode in a set of data. There can also be no mode if no values or results occur more than once.

EXAMPLE

What is the mode for the spinner experiment?

The mode is the gray area. It occurred the most number of times when the spinner was spun.

EXAMPLE

What is the mode for Jimmy's survey?

The mode is pizza. It occurred the most number of times.

PRACTICE

1. Experiment to see which number on a number cube numbered 1 through 6 occurs the most. Roll a number cube 20 times. Write down the number that occurs on the top of the number cube.

   _____

   _____

   What is the mode? _____

2. Ask your classmates the following survey question: *"What is your favorite color?"* Write down the colors that your classmates give.

   _____

   _____

   _____

   What is the mode? _____

Organizing and Displaying Data

Once you have collected your data, it is important to **organize** and **display** it so that it can be used. The lists in the spinner experiment and survey question examples are fine, but they are hard to use. Charts and graphs display the data so it is easier to use. The title of the chart or graph will give you the main idea of the data that is represented in the chart or graph. The labels tell you what each column or row represents.

Tally charts

A **tally chart** is an easy way to organize and display your data. The tally marks show the number of times that each value occurs.

EXAMPLE

Here is the tally chart for Jimmy's survey question from page 166.

title ———→ **Third-Graders' Favorite Lunches**

Type of Lunch	Number of Students	
Pizza	ʈʜʟ I	6
Hot Dogs	III	3
Chili	I	1
Spaghetti	II	2
Hamburgers	III	3
Soup	ʈʜʟ	5

label ———→ (Type of Lunch / Number of Students) ←——— label

KEY
| = 1
ʈʜʟ = 5

PRACTICE

1. How many of the third-graders said that soup is their favorite lunch?

_____

2. What did the least number of third-graders say was their favorite lunch?

_____

3. What two things did 3 third-graders say was their favorite lunch?

_____

Directions: For Numbers 4 through 6, use the data you collected in the number cube experiment on page 167.

4. Make a tally chart of the data.

5. Which numbers, if any, occurred the same number of times?

_____

6. Which number(s) occurred the least number of times? _____

Directions: For Numbers 7 through 9, use the data you collected in the favorite color survey on page 167.

7. Make a tally chart of the data.

8. Which colors, if any, did the same number of students say were their favorite?

_____

9. Put the colors in order starting with the color that the greatest number of students said was their favorite and ending with the color that the least number of students said was their favorite.

_____

_____

Pictographs

A **pictograph** uses pictures to show information. Use the **KEY** to help you figure out the number of times that each value from the pictograph occurs.

EXAMPLE

Three students are in charge of sending out invitations for a class party. This pictograph shows how many invitations Ty, Ann, and Zoe sent to their classmates.

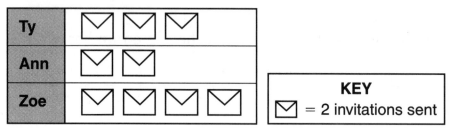

Invitations Sent to Classmates

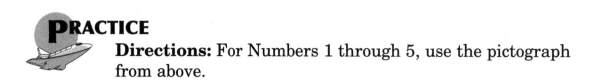

PRACTICE

Directions: For Numbers 1 through 5, use the pictograph from above.

1. Write a number pattern to show how many invitations Zoe sent.

_____

2. How many invitations has Ann sent? _____

3. Who has sent the most invitations? _____

4. How many invitations were sent altogether? _____

5. What is the main idea of this graph?_____

_____

Directions: Use the tally chart to answer Numbers 6 through 9.

This tally chart shows how many milk shakes, sodas, hot dogs, and hamburgers were sold during one month at Hamburger Bob's.

Item Sold	Number Sold	
Milk Shakes	~~IIII~~ ~~IIII~~ ~~IIII~~ ~~IIII~~ ~~IIII~~ ~~IIII~~	30
Sodas	~~IIII~~ ~~IIII~~ ~~IIII~~ ~~IIII~~ ~~IIII~~ ~~IIII~~ ~~IIII~~ ~~IIII~~	40
Hot Dogs	~~IIII~~ ~~IIII~~ ~~IIII~~ ~~IIII~~ ~~IIII~~ ~~IIII~~ ~~IIII~~ ~~IIII~~ ~~IIII~~ ~~IIII~~ ~~IIII~~ ~~IIII~~	60
Hamburgers	~~IIII~~ ~~IIII~~ ~~IIII~~ ~~IIII~~ ~~IIII~~ ~~IIII~~ ~~IIII~~ ~~IIII~~ ~~IIII~~ ~~IIII~~ ~~IIII~~ ~~IIII~~ ~~IIII~~ ~~IIII~~ ~~IIII~~ ~~IIII~~	80

KEY
| = 1
~~IIII~~ = 5

6. Make a pictograph of the data. Use the symbol found in the key in your pictograph.

Milk Shakes	
Sodas	
Hot Dogs	
Hamburgers	

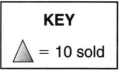

KEY

△ = 10 sold

7. How many more sodas were sold than milk shakes? _____

8. How many milk shakes, sodas, hot dogs, and hamburgers were sold altogether?

_____

9. What do you think the next person will buy from Hamburger Bob's, a hamburger or a hot dog? Explain your answer.

_____

_____

Bar graphs

A **bar graph** uses thick bars to compare information. The bars can go up and down or left and right. Be sure to check the labels on the graph.

EXAMPLE

The third-graders at Lucas Elementary collected newspapers during the school year. This bar graph shows how many pounds of newspapers the third-graders collected each month.

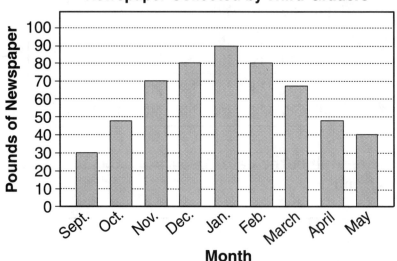

PRACTICE

Directions: Use the bar graph above to answer Numbers 1 through 4.

1. How many pounds of newspaper were collected in December?

_____

2. During which month was the most newspaper collected?

_____

3. What is the label along the side of the graph?

_____

4. What is the label along the bottom of the graph?

_____

Directions: Collect data about the eye color of your classmates. Then use the data to answer Numbers 5 through 8.

5. Fill in this tally chart with your data.

Color of Eyes	Number of Students
Brown	
Blue	
Green	
Hazel	
Other	

6. Make a horizontal bar graph of the data.

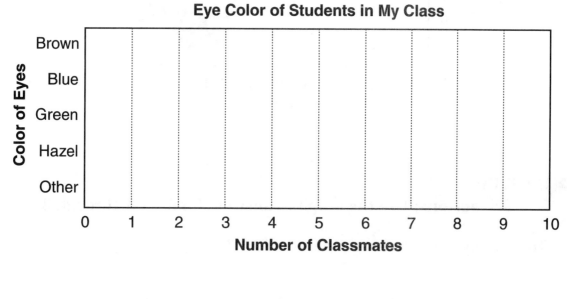

7. What is the mode of your data? _____

8. If a new student were to join your class tomorrow, what do you think his or her eye color would be? Explain your answer.

_____

_____

Line graphs

A **line graph** uses points and lines to show how data has changed over a period of time. Be sure to read the title and labels to determine the information in the graph.

EXAMPLE

Here is a line graph.

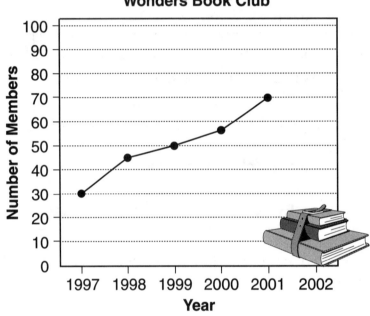

Members of the Reading Wonders Book Club

PRACTICE

Directions: Use the graph to answer Numbers 1 through 3.

1. How many members were there in 1999? _____

2. What is the main idea of the graph?

   _____

3. How many members do you think the Reading Wonders Book Club had in 2002? Explain your answer.

   _____

Line plots

A **line plot** uses marks to show the number of times that each value occurs.

 EXAMPLE

In their first 6 seasons, the Panthers won 7, 12, 7, 4, 8, and 7 games. Here is a line plot that shows the data.

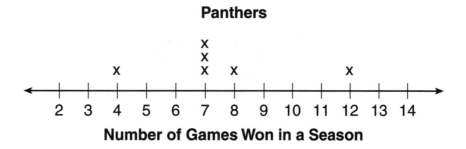

Panthers

Number of Games Won in a Season

Each X on the plot shows a season that the Panthers won that number of games.

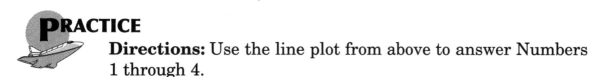 **PRACTICE**

Directions: Use the line plot from above to answer Numbers 1 through 4.

1. What is the mode of the data? _____

2. How many times did the Panthers win 8 games in a season?

_____

3. How many times did the Panthers win 6 games? _____

4. What is the most number of games that the Panthers have won in a season?

_____

Directions: For Numbers 5 through 9, record the outside temperature once a day for 15 school days.

5. Make a tally chart of your temperatures.

6. Make a line plot of your data.

7. What is the mode of your data? _____

8. What was the highest temperature that you recorded? _____

9. What was the lowest temperature that you recorded? _____

Circle graphs

A **circle graph** (also called a **pie chart**) shows how different parts make up a whole. You can compare the parts to each other and to the whole.

EXAMPLE

This circle graph shows the number of animals seen by Dr. Redstone, the veterinarian. You can see that about $\frac{1}{2}$ of the animals are dogs, $\frac{1}{4}$ are cats, and $\frac{1}{4}$ are other animals.

Dr. Redstone's Patients

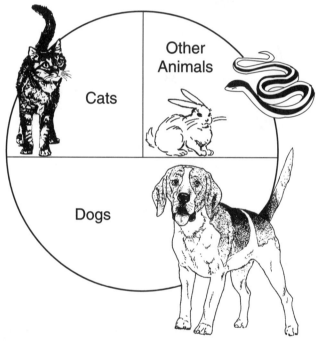

PRACTICE

Directions: Use the circle graph above to answer Numbers 1 and 2.

1. Dr. Redstone has seen 40 dogs. About how many cats and other animals has she seen altogether? Explain your answer.

_____

_____

2. Dr. Redstone has seen 40 dogs. About how many cats has she seen? Explain your answer.

_____

_____

Directions: Use the circle graph to answer Numbers 3 through 7.

Raj asked his classmates to name their favorite class, then he made a circle graph based on what they told him.

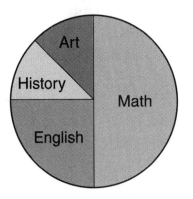

3. Which class was the favorite of the most students? _____

4. What two classes together are the favorite of about $\frac{1}{4}$ of the students?

_____

5. What would be a good title for the graph?

_____

6. Which class was the favorite of about $\frac{1}{4}$ of the students? _____

7. Raj has 24 classmates. About how many of them said their favorite class is math?

_____

TEST YOUR SKILLS

Directions: For Numbers 1 and 2, use this information.

Pete has a bag that has four blocks inside it. One block is blue, one is red, one is yellow, and one is black. He picked a block out of the bag without looking, recorded the color, and put it back into the bag. He did this a total of ten times. Here is a list of the colors that he picked:

red, black, yellow, blue, black, black, blue, black, red, blue

1. Which tally chart shows Pete's picks correctly recorded?

A.

Outcome	Tally	Number
Blue	II	2
Red	IIII	4
Yellow	III	3
Black	I	1

B.

Outcome	Tally	Number
Blue	I	1
Red	II	2
Yellow	III	3
Black	IIII	4

C.

Outcome	Tally	Number
Blue	III	3
Red	II	2
Yellow	I	1
Black	IIII	4

D.

Outcome	Tally	Number
Blue	IIII	4
Red	I	1
Yellow	III	3
Black	II	2

2. Which bar graph correctly displays Pete's data?

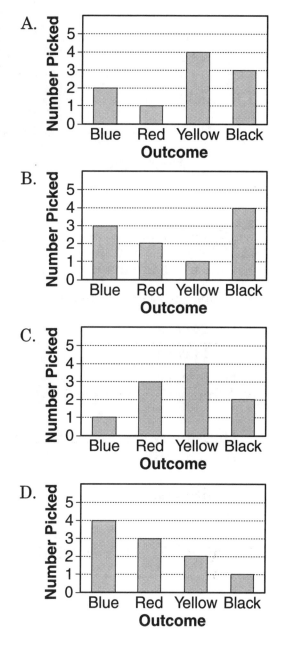

Directions: Use this information to answer Numbers 3 and 4.

This bar graph shows the number of cars that used the drive-through at Lucy's BBQ in a 3-hour time period.

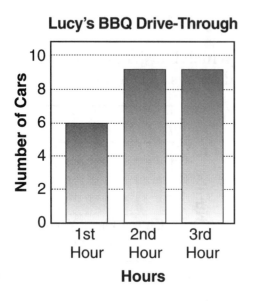

Lucy's BBQ Drive-Through

3. What is the total number of cars that used the drive-through?

   A. 21 cars
   B. 22 cars
   C. 23 cars
   D. 24 cars

4. How many cars used the drive-through in the 2nd hour?

   A. 6 cars
   B. 8 cars
   C. 9 cars
   D. 10 cars

Directions: Use this information to answer Numbers 5 and 6.

Hazel took a survey of which roller coaster students like the best. The results are found in this pictograph.

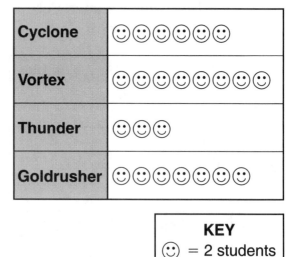

Number of Students Who Liked Each Roller Coaster

KEY
☺ = 2 students

5. What is the mode of the data?

   A. Cyclone
   B. Vortex
   C. Thunder
   D. Goldrusher

6. How many more students liked Cyclone than Thunder?

   A. 3 students
   B. 4 students
   C. 6 students
   D. 9 students

Directions: Use this information to answer Numbers 7 and 8.

Some students set up an experiment to see how fast water will evaporate. The results are displayed in this line graph.

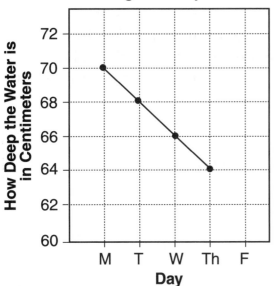

Wading Pool Experiment

7. What was the depth of the water in the pool on Wednesday?

   A. 65 cm

   B. 66 cm

   C. 67 cm

   D. 68 cm

8. If the pattern in the graph continues, how deep will the water be on Friday?

   A. 60 cm

   B. 62 cm

   C. 64 cm

   D. 66 cm

Directions: Use this information to answer Numbers 9 and 10.

Sasha asked her classmates what their favorite after-school activity is. Her results are found in this circle graph.

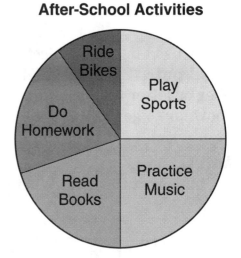

After-School Activities

9. Which of these activities did the most classmates say is their favorite?

   A. ride bikes

   B. read books

   C. do homework

   D. practice music

10. Which activity did the least number of classmates say is their favorite?

   A. ride bikes

   B. read books

   C. play sports

   D. do homework

Grids and Time Lines

Grids and time lines are two other types of graphs. Grids show location and time lines show the order of events.

Grids

A **grid** is used to locate objects. Each object's location is given by an **ordered pair**. (2, 8) and (G, 4) are examples of ordered pairs. The first number or letter tells you how far to go across. The second number tells you how far to go up.

EXAMPLE

Look at the grid. Where is the calculator located?

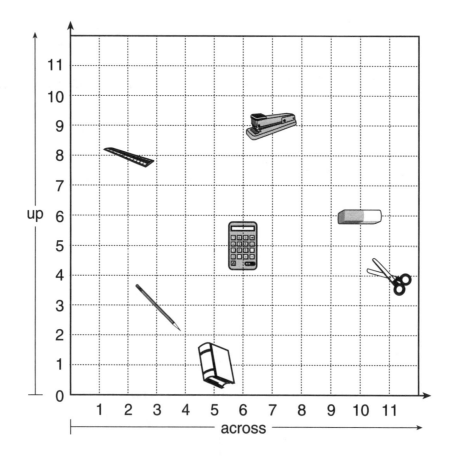

To get to the calculator you have to go across to 6. Then you go up to 5. The calculator is located at (6, 5).

EXAMPLE

What object is located at (10, 6)?

Go across to 10. Then go up to 6.

The eraser is located at (10, 6).

PRACTICE

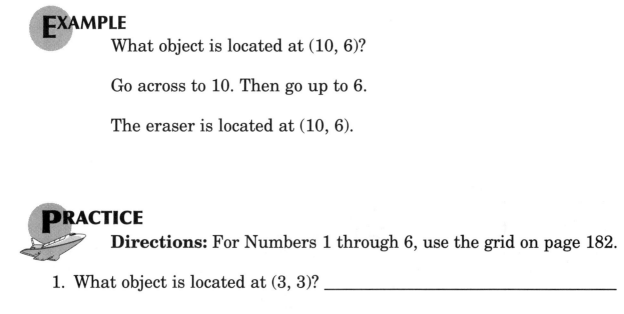

Directions: For Numbers 1 through 6, use the grid on page 182.

1. What object is located at (3, 3)? _____

2. Where is the ruler located? _____

3. Draw a triangle at (4, 6).

4. What object will you find if you move 11 units across and 4 units up?

   _____

   What is the ordered pair? _____

5. Where is the book located? _____

6. Where is the stapler located?

   A. (6, 10)
   B. (10, 6)
   C. (7, 9)
   D. (9, 7)

Sometimes locations are described using letters and numbers.

EXAMPLE

Look at the grid below. Where is the school located?

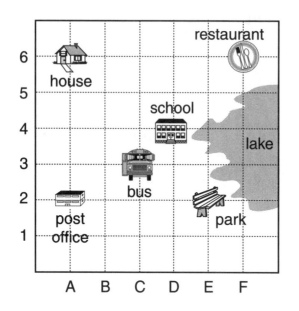

To get to the school, you go across to D. Then you go up to 4.
The school is located at (D, 4).

PRACTICE

Directions: Use the grid above to answer Numbers 1 through 5.

1. What object is located at (A, 2)? _____

2. What is the location of the restaurant? _____

3. Draw a tree at (C, 5).

4. What object is located at (E, 2)? _____

5. What is the location of the bus?

   A. (D, 3)
   B. (D, 4)
   C. (C, 3)
   D. (C, 4)

Time lines

A **time line** shows the order in which events happen. A time line is like a number line. The order of the events is from left to right.

EXAMPLE

Jonah kept track of the things he did one Saturday. This is what he did:

9:00 A.M. – watched cartoons

10:00 A.M. – raked leaves

11:30 A.M. – rode bikes with Owen

12:30 P.M. – ate lunch at Simon's

1:00 P.M. – went to the movies with Tyler

He made this time line to show the events of that Saturday.

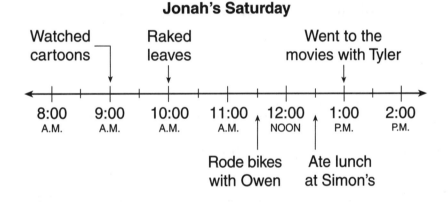

Notice the time is ordered from left to right. The events are listed and point to the times when they happened.

PRACTICE

Directions: Use the time line below to answer Numbers
1 through 3.

This time line shows some of the things Danielle did on her vacation.

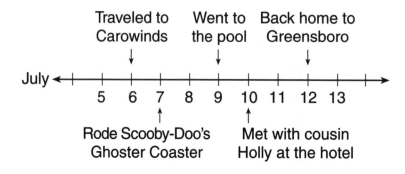

Danielle's July

1. When did Danielle go to the pool? _____

2. When did Danielle meet her cousin Holly at the hotel?

   _____

3. What happened on July 7? _____

4. Write down 5 things that you did one day and the times you did them.

   _____

   _____

   _____

   _____

   _____

   Make a time line that shows what you did that day.

TEST YOUR SKILLS

Directions: Use the grid below to answer Numbers 1 through 4.

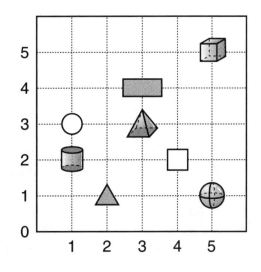

1. What object is located at (2, 1)?

   A.

   B.

   C.

   D.

2. Where is the ◯ located?

   A. (1, 3)
   B. (3, 3)
   C. (2, 3)
   D. (3, 1)

3. What object is located at (5, 5)?

   A.

   B.

   C.

   D.

4. Where is the 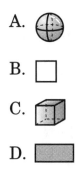 located?

   A. (3, 4)
   B. (1, 3)
   C. (3, 3)
   D. (4, 3)

Directions: Use the time line below to answer Numbers 5 through 8.

This time line shows the years that seven U.S. presidents took office from 1969 to 2001.

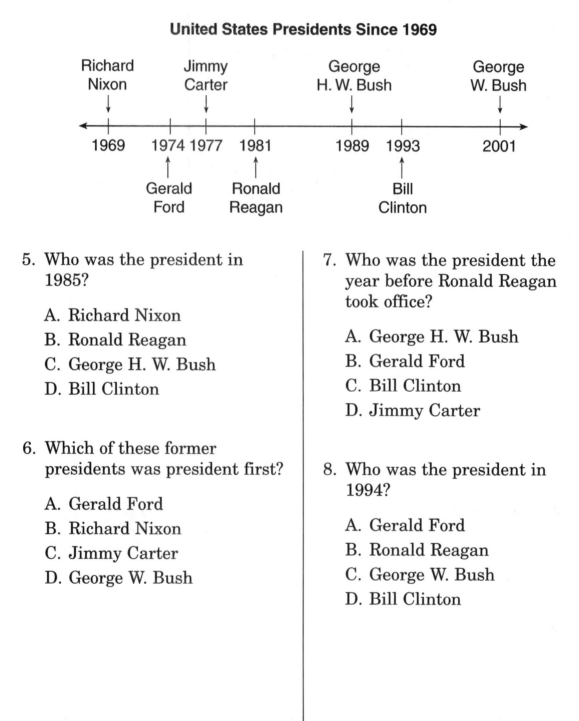

United States Presidents Since 1969

5. Who was the president in 1985?

   A. Richard Nixon
   B. Ronald Reagan
   C. George H. W. Bush
   D. Bill Clinton

6. Which of these former presidents was president first?

   A. Gerald Ford
   B. Richard Nixon
   C. Jimmy Carter
   D. George W. Bush

7. Who was the president the year before Ronald Reagan took office?

   A. George H. W. Bush
   B. Gerald Ford
   C. Bill Clinton
   D. Jimmy Carter

8. Who was the president in 1994?

   A. Gerald Ford
   B. Ronald Reagan
   C. George W. Bush
   D. Bill Clinton

 **Lesson 16**

Probability

Probability is how likely it is that an event will happen. Sometimes more than one event happens at the same time. Then it is important to be able to list all the arrangements or combinations of the events.

Probability

You can predict that the probability of one event happening is **more likely**, **less likely**, or **equally likely** to happen than a different event.

XAMPLES

Is it more likely, less likely, or equally likely for the spinner to stop on a white area?

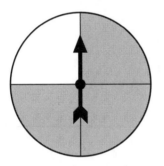

The spinner is divided into four areas that are each the same size. There is only 1 area that is white, and there are 3 areas that are gray.

Since $1 < 3$, it is less likely for the spinner to stop on a white area.

Is it more likely, less likely, or equally likely for the spinner above to stop on a gray area?

Since $3 > 1$, it is more likely for the spinner to stop on a gray area.

➡ **TIP:** Two events are **equally likely** if they have the same chance of occurring.

PRACTICE

Directions: For Numbers 1 through 6, write whether the event listed is more likely, less likely, or equally likely to occur.

1. drawing a ● out of the bag without looking

_____

2. the spinner stopping on the striped area

_____

3. flipping a coin and it landing heads up _____

4. rolling a 3 on a number cube numbered 1 through 6

_____

5. guessing correctly on a true/false question you don't know the answer to

_____

6. guessing correctly on a multiple-choice question with 4 choices you don't know the answer to

_____

Arrangements and Combinations

Arrangements and combinations show the number of ways that things can occur.

Arrangements

An **arrangement** is the ordering of a set of objects.

EXAMPLE

How many ways can you arrange a circle, a triangle, and a square? List the different arrangements.

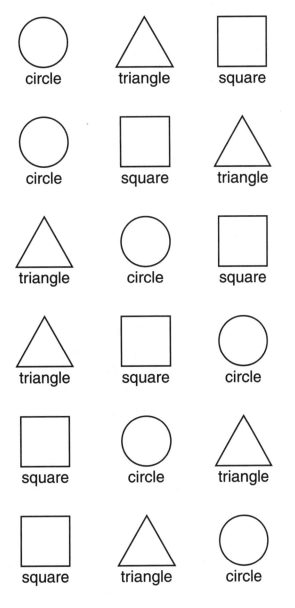

They are 6 ways to arrange a circle, a triangle, and a square.

PRACTICE

1. List the ways that Ginny, Mark, and Chloe can stand in line.

    There are _____ ways Ginny, Mark, and Chloe can stand in line.

2. Tony has a raisin and a grape. List the ways that Tony can eat them one at a time.

    There are _____ ways Tony can eat a raisin and a grape.

3. Draw and list the ways that these figures can be arranged in a line so that the two that are striped are not next to each other.

    There are _____ ways the figures can be arranged.

Combinations

A **combination** is the way that different objects can be put together.
A **tree diagram** will help you to list the different combinations.

EXAMPLE

Katie wants to see a movie and read a book this weekend. She
has 2 movies and 3 books to choose from. Here are her choices:

Movie	Book
Mulan	*Sarah, Plain and Tall*
The Great Mouse Detective	*Charlotte's Web*
	Henry Huggins

How many combinations of a movie and a book does Katie have
to choose from? Make a tree diagram to list the combinations.

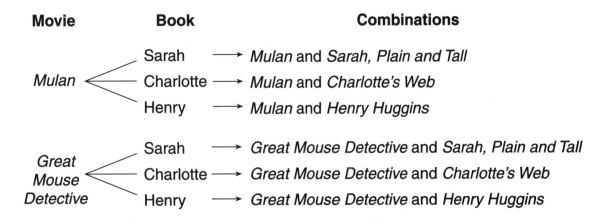

Katie has 6 combinations of a movie and a book to choose from.

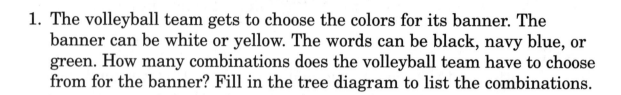

PRACTICE

1. The volleyball team gets to choose the colors for its banner. The banner can be white or yellow. The words can be black, navy blue, or green. How many combinations does the volleyball team have to choose from for the banner? Fill in the tree diagram to list the combinations.

Banner	**Words**	**Combinations**
	black ⟶	_____
white	navy blue ⟶	_____
	green ⟶	_____
	black ⟶	_____
yellow	navy blue ⟶	_____
	green ⟶	_____

The volleyball team has _____ combinations to choose from.

2. Jenny is going to flip a coin twice. She will record the side that lands up. How many combinations are there for Jenny to record? Make a tree diagram to list the combinations.

Jenny could record _____ combinations.

3. Luke has a blue jacket, 2 shirts (1 blue and 1 white), and 2 pair of pants (1 tan and 1 blue) that he can wear today. How many combinations does Luke have to choose from if he wears a jacket, a shirt, and a pair of pants? Make a tree diagram to list the combinations.

Luke has _____ combinations to choose from.

TEST YOUR SKILLS

Directions: For Numbers 1 and 2, use this information.

Eli is making a peanut butter and jelly sandwich for lunch. He will use 1 kind of peanut butter and 1 kind of jelly. He has the following choices to put on his bread:

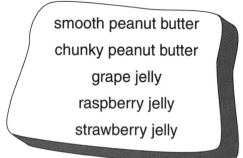

smooth peanut butter

chunky peanut butter

grape jelly

raspberry jelly

strawberry jelly

1. How many combinations does Eli have to choose from for his sandwich?

    A.   5
    B.   6
    C.   8
    D. 10

2. Eli's mom told him that he also has 2 kinds of bread to choose from: white and rye. Now how many combinations does Eli have to choose from for his sandwich?

    A.   6
    B. 12
    C. 16
    D. 18

3. From which bag is it **more likely** to pick a ?

    A.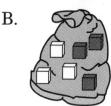

    B.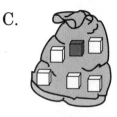

    C.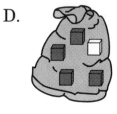

    D.

4. Thomas checked three books out from the library. How many different ways can Thomas arrange to read the books?

    A. 3
    B. 4
    C. 5
    D. 6

5. On which spinner is the
   ➤——➤ **less likely** to stop
   on the striped area?

   A.

   B.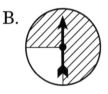

   C.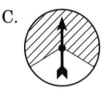

   D.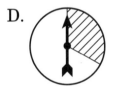

6. Ralph's family has the choice of
   visiting Washington, D.C., Cape
   Hatteras National Seashore,
   or Hilton Head Island, South
   Carolina this summer. They
   also have the choice of going
   in June, July, or August. How
   many combinations of one
   place to visit and one month
   does Ralph's family have to
   choose from?

   A. 9
   B. 8
   C. 7
   D. 6

7. How many different ways are
   there to arrange the letters
   A, B, and C?

   A. 6
   B. 8
   C. 12
   D. 15

8. There are 24 pencils in a box.
   Ten are yellow, 9 are blue,
   3 are purple, and 2 are red.
   You are going to pick one pencil
   from the box without looking.
   Which of these statements
   about the pencils is true?

   A. The chance of you picking a
      yellow or blue pencil is **less
      likely** than the chance of
      you picking a purple or red.
   B. The chance of you picking
      a blue or red pencil is
      more likely than the
      chance of you picking a
      yellow or purple.
   C. The chance of you picking
      a yellow or red pencil is
      equally likely to the
      chance of you picking a
      blue or purple.
   D. The chance of you picking
      a yellow or purple pencil
      is **equally likely** to the
      chance of you picking a
      blue or red.

APPENDIX

Buckle Down Learning
Standards and Skills
for Mathematics,
Level 3

Buckle Down Learning Standards and Skills for Mathematics, Level 3

Buckle Down on Mathematics, Level 3, is based on learning standards and skills common to Grade 3 mathematics curricula in the United States. The workbook teaches problem-solving and test-taking strategies that are generalizable to any test. The following table matches the standards and skills with the workbook lessons in which they are addressed.

Learning Standards and Skills		*Buckle Down* Lesson(s)
Standard 1	**Number Sense, Numeration, and Numerical Operations: The student will model, identify, and compute with numbers.**	
Skill 1.1	Use place value to read, write, and describe the value of whole numbers.	1
Skill 1.2	Compare and order whole numbers.	1
Skill 1.3	Identify odd and even numbers.	1
Skill 1.4	Use fraction names to describe fractional parts of whole objects or sets of objects.	2
Skill 1.5	Compare and order fractions.	2
Skill 1.6	Add and subtract to solve problems involving whole numbers.	3
Skill 1.7	Use the identity and commutative properties for addition and multiplication.	3
Skill 1.8	Recall and use multiplication facts.	3
Skill 1.9	Demonstrate an understanding of division and its relationship to multiplication.	3
Skill 1.10	Solve problems involving addition, subtraction, and multiplication using a variety of strategies.	4
Skill 1.11	Identify missing or extraneous information in problem-solving situations.	4
Skill 1.12	Use estimation to determine solutions.	4

Learning Standards and Skills		Buckle Down Lesson(s)
Standard 2	**Spatial Sense, Measurement, and Geometry: The student will recognize and use standard units of measurement and basic geometric properties.**	
Skill 2.1	Estimate and measure length, weight, and capacity using metric and customary units.	5–7
Skill 2.2	Compare units within the same measurement system.	5–7
Skill 2.3	Determine the value of sets of coins and make change.	8
Skill 2.4	Use digital and analog clocks to tell time.	9
Skill 2.5	Use a thermometer to measure temperature.	9
Skill 2.6	Name, describe, draw, and compare plane and solid figures.	10, 11
Skill 2.7	Identify congruent shapes.	10
Skill 2.8	Identify lines of symmetry in shapes.	10
Skill 2.9	Determine perimeter and area.	10
Skill 2.10	Solve real-world problems using measurement concepts.	5–10
Standard 3	**Patterns, Relationships, and Functions: The student will describe and analyze a variety of patterns, relations, and functions.**	
Skill 3.1	Organize objects or ideas into groups.	12
Skill 3.2	Use Venn diagrams to show relationships.	12
Skill 3.3	Analyze and describe patterns.	13
Skill 3.4	Extend and create patterns.	13
Skill 3.5	Use patterns to make predictions and solve problems.	13
Standard 4	**Data, Probability, and Statistics: The student will demonstrate an understanding of data collection and analysis, graphing, and probability.**	
Skill 4.1	Gather, organize, and display data using charts and graphs.	14
Skill 4.2	Describe data using mode.	14
Skill 4.3	Interpret charts and graphs.	14
Skill 4.4	Use ordered pairs to locate points and plot positions on a coordinate grid.	15
Skill 4.5	Use time lines to display sequences of events.	15
Skill 4.6	Describe the probability of chance events.	16
Skill 4.7	List all possible arrangements (permutations) of a given set of objects.	16

Notes

Notes